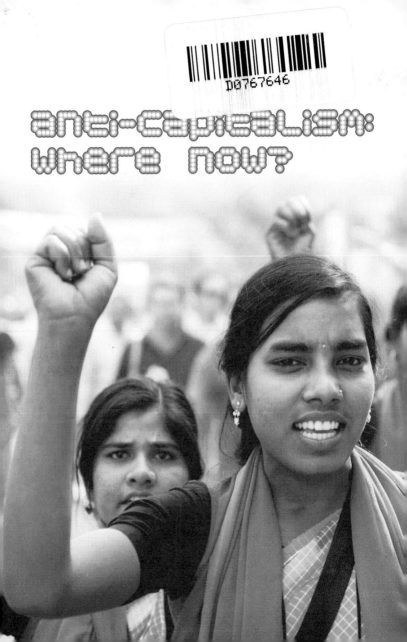

anti-capitalism: where now?

anti-capitalism: where now?

Edited by Hannah Dee

Bookmarks *b* publications

Anti-Capitalism: Where Now?

Published October 2004
Bookmarks Publications
1 Bloomsbury Street
London WC1B 3QE

The material in this book is free for non-profit
organisation to use, otherwise: Copyright Bookmarks
Publications Ltd

ISBN 1 898876 80 0

Designed by Peter Robinson
Translations by Tom Behan and Andy Brown
Printed by Cambridge Printing

Cover and page 1 pictures:
World Social Forum, Mumbai, India, January 2004.
Jess Hurd www.reportdigital.co.uk

Contents

un autre monde est possible

otro mundo es posible

another world is possible

Opening Rally of the World Social Forum in Mumbai, India, 2004
Picture: Jess Hurd www.reportdigital.co.uk

Introduction

Consider what we have achieved.

We have succeeded in launching a serious and sustained challenge to a system which puts profit before people and war before peace. We have opposed this agenda in every corner of the globe, at every opportunity presented. World leaders can no longer meet without mass protests organised on an unprecedented scale. We have sent a signal to them and ourselves that we will not be turned back. We will not be dissuaded. We do not recognise their authority, where that authority brings so much suffering and waste. We have set a new agenda and we aim to fulfil it.

This collection of writings, from some of the key activists in our movement, charts the development of anti-capitalism, from the battle against the WTO in Seattle 1998, through to Mumbai 2004. The central theme of this book is where now for our movement? As Vittorio Agnoletto, newly elected Italian MEP, has said, the movement can no longer be thought of in terms of 'simple acts of resistance'. Our movement has come from the failure of neo-liberalism to win us over, its creation of huge inequality, and finally, its recourse to war. That is where it's come from. We now need to look at where it's going. We have declared that another world is possible. In this book we debate how we move towards that alternative.

Haidi Giuliani, the mother of anti-capitalist protester Carlo Giuliani, who was killed by the Italian police in 2001, writes about the fight for justice, against state repression and violence. She refers to the 'Genoa generation'. These are the people who she meets every day on her travels 'from city to city, from country to country, taking part in rallies, meetings and festivals'. Carlo's father, Giuliano Giuliani, talks about the ways his son politicised him, above all through 'the culture of doing'. 'The culture of talking is quite right and correct,' he says, 'but apart from talking we need to do things as well.'

In the 'The Whole World Over', Billy Hayes, general secretary of the Communication Workers Union (UK), talks about the way globalisation crushes workers in both the rich and the poor countries. He stresses the importance of the alliance between trade unionists and anti-capitalists for the success of both domestic and international struggles.

The anti-capitalist movement played a central role in building the global movement against war. This movement politicised millions, with many beginning to make the connection between corporate globalisation and imperialism. It was at the ESF in Florence that the call for a global day of action on 15 February was made. On that historic day 20 million marched worldwide, marking the arrival of what has been described as 'the world's second superpower'. Believing they could defy this movement and survive, Bush, Blair and Aznar went ahead with their war and the bloody occupation of Iraq.

So, while the anti-capitalist movement has won some important victories, Susan George notes that the other side remain 'in the saddle'. In 'Taking the Movement Forward' she argues that 'we have identified and interpreted the targets—the point, however, is to hit them.' So how do we do this? We need to begin by asking the right questions: 'Where is the adversary weakest?' 'Which of our campaigns are most likely to touch raw and exposed establishment nerves?' 'What victory, if achieved, would provide the greatest good for the greatest number and the best launching pad for future campaigns?'

In 'Join the Global Mutiny' Naomi Klein insists that opposition to the occupation in Iraq must remain a central organising focus for the movement. This is something which features in many of the contributions to this book. Klein argues that the neo-liberal project is at its most brutal and bloody in Iraq, but that Iraq is also its weakest link. We must use this fact to mobilise since, although 'the damage of this war cannot be undone...at least the men who waged it can be taught that it doesn't pay to set the world on fire and try to turn a profit off the ashes.'

But what are our strategies? Even if within the movement we are clear about who our enemies are, there is real debate about how to confront them. In 'The Future of the Anti-Capitalist Movement', Alex Callinicos talks about the different approaches to confronting US power and neo-liberal globalisation. He also addresses one of the most prominent questions in the book: How do we organise ourselves, what is the role of the Social Forum and do political parties have any place within it?

Prabir Purkayastha of the Delhi Science Forum draws on his experience in organising the World Social Forum in Mumbai to consider: Are the social forums simply a space for debate or for organising our struggles, or can they involve both? Should they be seen as a temporary bodies or something more permanent? What about democracy and the role of leadership and political parties in the movement?

One of the tragic features of this period is the way so many social democratic parties have been elected on a wave of opposition to neo-liberalism, only to embrace it. Deputy Luciana Genro is one of four MPs expelled from the PT (Workers Party) for voting against Lula's government plans to cut pensions. She places the events that led to their expulsion in the context of wider struggles taking place across Latin America, and describes their strategy for building a left alternative—P-SOL, the socialism and freedom party.

One of the most popular slogans thrown up by the movement is 'Another world is possible.' But what would that world look like, and how far will we need to go to achieve it? Can we change the institutions and structures of capitalism, or will they have to be overthrown? In 'Beyond Capitalism' Michael Albert offers a series of challenging questions for those seeking economic alternatives to capitalism, and proposes an alternative in what he calls 'participatory economics'.

This book brings together some of the key questions and debates within the movement, and tries to provide some answers. In doing so we hope it will contribute to the development of our movement, as it continues to strengthen and grow.

Hannah Dee, Bookmarks Publications
publications@bookmarks.uk.com

Haidi Giuliani is a retired school teacher and trade union activist.

Giuliano Giuliani is a retired full time union officer of the CGIL trade union federation and now runs a local co-operative in Genoa.

Giuliano and Haidi Giuliani are the parents of Carlo Giuliani who was murdered by police during the Genoa demonstrations in 2001. They spend much of their time campaigning for justice for Carlo and the victims of wrongful arrest and police violence in the Genoa demonstrations.
www.piazzacarlogiuliani.org /
www.vertiagiustia

genoa: talking about my generations

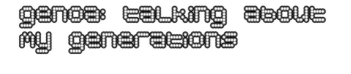

Haidi Giuliani

I remember when I was a teacher I often used to talk with my class about rights: rights that had been denied to so many kids of their own age, such as a home to live in and grow up in, a decent education, a family, a homeland. So many kids, even at a very young age, are forced to work and treated like slaves, or are forced to live every day with the fear of war or the violence created by 'them'.

Children have a clear and natural sense of justice— they don't compromise. They can't understand how someone can get rich through somebody else's suffering, or how others can adapt themselves according to the desires of the powerful, hurting the weakest in society so as to grab the few crumbs which fall from the table, reducing themselves to servants in the illusion that they're sitting down to eat the same meal.

The years pass, and by now many of those grown-up children no longer remember the injustices suffered by such a large part of humanity. On the contrary—I suppose the best thing is that our young people don't find out too much about this, that they don't get to the bottom of certain issues, that they just think about a career and enjoying themselves with the limited means offered by a limited culture.

Television ought just to entertain, as uncritically as possible. Newspapers are fine as long as they write mainly about football and crime (it's always a relief reading about people worse off than we are)—not too much politics though—and what there is should be toned down.

Despite all this, however, many young and not so young people have kept a clear sense of justice. There are loads of them, and I meet them every day travelling from city to city, from country to country, taking part in rallies, meetings and festivals.

This is 'the Genoa generation'—who came to my city three years ago to say no to the eight representatives of the world's richest countries. The G8 met in a kind of fortress, a 'red zone' fenced off and separated from the rest of humanity, surrounded by guards armed to the teeth. They were meeting to agree on a new economic policy and to decide how to manage the new global market.

That varied generation of environmentalists, Christians involved in community work, Communists, anarchists, scouts, trade unionists, activists from social centres, radical youth groups—had all met in Genoa to deny 'them'—the G8 leaders, the right, even if they were elected, to make decisions on behalf of 6 billion people and an entire planet. They wanted those who were never heard to get a hearing. They said that climate, the food chain, energy sources, the global rules of the economy, concerned everyone—you can't exclude Africa, Latin America and the Far East. You cannot destroy, in the name of profit, what future generations might want to preserve!

This is what they were saying. And the incredible thing was that they all said it together.

We all know what happened next—ferocious repression. Stalls run by Christian activists selling books and handicrafts were smashed up by the police. Young people and nuns, already stunned, were beaten with truncheons. Everybody was a target when the police charged: doctors and nurses who were tending the injured, journalists, patients inside ambulances. Those who fell over, or who didn't run away fast enough, were kicked and beaten with odds of ten police to one demonstrator. Bones were broken and teeth were knocked out—people were injured all over their bodies. They fired CS canisters down on the march from helicopters, aiming indiscriminately— pregnant women and children were not spared. At the end of two days the balance sheet was one dead and hundreds injured, some of them very seriously. But then, just when it all seemed to be at an end, the police attacked a left wing radio station, the press centre of the Genoa Social Forum (the organisation that coordinated the demonstrations), and smashed their way into the Diaz school at night, injuring people who were still in their sleeping bags. They also fired tear gas at coaches leaving the city, and launched an attack on a hospital accident and emergency ward in order to take some of the injured into custody, where they got beaten up again. Often the police wouldn't even say who they had under arrest.

Nobody knew what the G8 leaders had decided. Everyone forgot about the important issues raised and discussed by the movement over the preceding weeks. Criticism of the police even came from the middle ground of politics. Comparisons were made with Pinochet's Chile. Foreign newspapers denounced the criminal actions of the Italian police. Some countries protested through their foreign ministries. The Italian government defended the police's behaviour, and responded to the criticisms and demands for explanations with cynicism and arrogance. Many police commanders, directly responsible for the violence, were promoted. But the demonstrations didn't stop—they just moved—in front of the police stations of many Italian cities and many Italian embassies around the world.

The attack on the Twin Towers in New York seemed to push these protests into the background. Meanwhile the government tried to equate the movement to terrorism and asked people to line up behind 'Western values'. But the protests didn't stop—on the contrary a period of massive demonstrations began. Many cities saw big marches, first against repression, then against the bombing of Afghanistan and finally against war in Iraq.

This spring in Genoa 26 demonstrators from 2001 were brought to trial—26 scapegoats. They are accused of 'vandalism and looting', a crime for which a sentence of eight to 15 years is normally given. The Genoa Social Forum and its spokespersons reconvened and stated:

Genoa is an open wound in our democratic conscience. The whole of Italy and the world know that something very serious and unacceptable happened over those two days. In effect political and civil rights were suspended so as to smash a wonderful example of mass action and protest.

What is needed is that the police chiefs and political leaders who planned and carried out the repression answer to the whole country for their actions, so that faith in our democracy can be restored. We oppose any attempt to rewrite history along the lines of the city being devastated by violent demonstrators—on the contrary it was demonstrators' resistance that stopped the balance sheet becoming even worse. We believe that only by examining the overall context of what happened will it be possible to assess the charges some demonstrators are now facing.

They were totally ignored.

In the early summer the first court hearings start concerning the violent police raid on the Diaz school. Lorenzo Guadagnucci of the Comitato Verità e Giustizia per Genova (the Genoa Truth and Justice Committee) writes:

All the investigations, charges, and mountains of accusations seem not to bother senior police officers, to not speak of ministers and leaders of political parties—whether in government or opposition. All of them want to keep very quiet. Newspapers show a minimal amount of interest—indeed you need to go to Britain and read the **Guardian** *to find a national newspaper that sets aside a whole page to deal with the opening hearing on events in the Diaz school. Television news bulletins about it last a few seconds, and it is presented as merely a legal matter—heaven forbid any talk about the political and ethical questions the whole case raises. With the revelations that emerge from the hearings nobody asks how credible the police is as an institution. The need to re-establish the primacy of constitutional rights doesn't occur to anyone… In September the number of trials will increase— there will be the first hearings about events in the Bolzaneto barracks.[1] But the overall situation will far worsen in terms* *of charges against those who organise demonstrations or take part in them—with the opening of the trial in Cosenza against 13 activists of the Rete del Sud Ribelle (the Rebel South Network). The charges are spine-chilling: 'political conspiracy', 'violent subversion of the economic order', 'subversive association'…Whether you look at Genoa, Cosenza or Naples,[2] this is a historical period without any dignity whatsoever. Thanks to widespread complicity, the common-sense view today is that what is happening in courthouses up and down the country isn't important or serious. There's a strong wish to forget about the humiliation suffered by the hundreds of thousands of people who took part in demonstrations in Naples and Genoa—indeed the humiliation of democracy itself. After attacking our bodies, they want to brainwash our minds. In this situation, the search for truth is the same thing as regaining our dignity.*

And what about the Genoa generation, and the movement? They're still around. They're a bit tired. They lose their voice a bit during election campaigns. Really they're like an underground river, suddenly bursting out in full flow. Once in a while you hear little stories about wonderful people who put all their time and energy into building bridges. And in support of these people, we're able to organise four separate meetings in one day, across a single city.

The great lesson of Genoa is difficult to absorb, to work out and to practise, but it's this: it is far easier to divide yourself into groups, sub-groups and sub-sub-groups. Whereas it is far harder to decide that what is at stake is big—so big that you need to discard any sense of exclusiveness, overcome the fear of losing your own identity, symbols and banners. Not only is it possible, it is necessary to come together over just a few clear but essential issues:

peace, sustainable development, and all those things which are already written in our constitutions—if only they hadn't become toilet paper for so long—if only we hadn't let it happen.

The 'Genoa generations' are still around. Sometimes they start stuttering a bit, just when you'd think the time has come to shout the loudest, because the Earth can't stand so much pain.

I can't avoid ending by remembering one of the far too many victims of repression and global war. In the words of film director Francesca Comencini:

This has been the great strength of Carlo Giuliani. With his life but also with his so unjust death, with his personality, with something of him that—despite the accusations and silences—has mysteriously been handed down intact to us, precisely and intimately. Carlo had wings and reached all of us. Carlo has given strength to me and many others—the strength to say, each in our own way, 'This isn't right.'

Haidi Giuliani

Notes

1 Many demonstrators who were arrested and then taken to this holding centre have subsequently accused the police of torture.

2 In March 2001, four months before the Genoa demonstration, police violently attacked an anti-OECD protest in Naples.

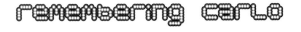

remembering carlo

Giuliano Giuliani

I am going to try and tell you some of the things that Carlo has taught me. He's actually brought me here to London—I've never been here before. I'm going to talk about what he taught me about justice, politics, the media and about war.

I always believed and I still believe in justice and the judiciary. But I think today I've got the duty and the right to talk about and criticise the acts of one single magistrate, one single judge. And here I'm reminded of a famous passage in a book by Victor Hugo. When Quasimodo gets arrested and is bought in front of a judge, in reality the judge has got a problem—he is deaf. But he manages to hide his deafness by reading all the trial documents very carefully and in great detail, learning them by heart in order to hide his problem. So he gets all his replies ready—he reads everything—so he's prepared in case he suddenly gets asked an unexpected kind of question. He's there and he's ready. The people who are watching think that he's either a bit stupid or very intelligent and well prepared. What Hugo says is that in any event the important thing in either case is that the integrity of the judiciary and the judge should be maintained. Because it is much better that a judge is either very stupid or very intelligent and learned, rather than being deaf. For us what happened with the killing of Carlo is that we got a deaf judge—deaf and blind who didn't want to understand a single thing about the case. He didn't want to see one single thing, and fell for all the lies about the stones you could see flying about on the video footage at the moment when Carlo was killed.[1] Carlo has therefore also taught me to doubt the seriousness and impartiality of judges.

What Carlo has taught me about politics is that what is most important isn't necessarily ideologies, but the ability to look at things concretely. And I'm reminded of a very dear friend of mine in Italy who died recently, Tom Benetollo, president of ARCI, a left wing cultural association, who once told this story about when he was young and first joined the Communist Party. When he went to his branch, an old worker who was branch secretary told him to be very wary about both reformism and 'maximalism' or extremism. He said that reformism means 'nothing now', but that extremism means 'everything never'! Carlo looked at things concretely: what was needed to be done, how it should be done, what everyone needed to do—that's what he thought about. That was his political lesson.

And he also taught me to mistrust the media. I always thought being a journalist must be a lovely profession. There can't be many better occupations than the job of being a journalist—a job where you can talk about things people understand, things that are happening, things that are real.

But how many journalists are there around the world who are simply servants for regimes—who have told us lies about Genoa, about the killing of Carlo, about the war, about ordinary people's living conditions. In Italy today we've still got journalists who say everything is lovely, everything's perfect. But in the last week of the month the consumption and buying of milk in supermarkets decreases hugely—there are people who haven't got the money at the end of the month to actually buy a pint of milk. Think about the photos of Piazza Alimonda, the square where Carlo died. There's a famous photo published by Reuters taken with a telephoto lens, which flattens perspective, in which Carlo appears to be threatening a police Land Rover. But there are a lot of other photos, taken with normal lenses and often from the side, that show you far more accurately the reality of what was happening. Yet this Reuters telephoto lens photo has been shown and reproduced tens of thousands of times around the world, and it appears as if Carlo is right on top of this police Land Rover. Yet you could count the publication of these other photos on the fingers of one hand. So I've not got much trust today in the media—I'm very critical of all of them. And I hope that with all that the movement is doing—we can defeat all these media lies. We've got one big enemy—that damned horrible box—that tries as hard as it can to turn us all into idiots! But carrying on with our activity, and talking to each other, we can rebuild public squares, forums if you like—forums for discussion, for pleasure, for living things how they really are, and not how they want us to believe things are.

Carlo looked at things concretely: what needed to be done. That was his political lesson

Giuliano Giuliani

Carlo also taught me to view war as the worst thing that exists. Many years ago we were at Remagen, a town on the river Rhine in Germany. There used to be a bridge over the Rhine that had been destroyed during the Second World War, and in the middle of the bridge they had built a museum of peace. There were three walls in this museum full of tiles, and on each of the tiles there was the date of a war that had begun in the world since 1945. If they had carried on putting these tiles up they probably would have covered the fourth wall in order to put all the dates on. Carlo said to me, 'Where's peace?' 'Where is it?' 'What's the point of building a museum of peace, if all these wars are breaking out all over the world?' 'Who is to blame for this?' This was during the wars in ex-Yugoslavia, and Carlo was saying to me the reason these wars were happening is because of the system, the rich, it is the multinationals who were to blame—this is what he was saying to me then. And I was saying, 'These are countries where ethnic groups have been fighting each other for 500 years. The Croats hate the Serbs. The Serbs hate the Bosnians. The Bosnians hate the Croats.' But while I would sit talking to him and going, 'Bla, bla, bla', Carlo went back to Genoa and collected food and blankets to send to refugees in Sarajevo.

One other thing he taught me was the culture of doing things. The culture of talking is quite right and correct, but apart from talking we need to do things as well. And we need a huge generosity—and he had this. I think he taught me, and everyone else, that against all the injustices in the world it is right to raise an 'extinguisher of injustice'[2] in protest, because this is a gesture of courage, generosity and love towards those who are suffering. This is what Carlo has taught me, and for this I still thank him to this day.

Giuliano Giuliani was speaking at Marxism 2004

Notes

1   The court hearings to investigate Carlo Giuliani's death found that the bullet that killed him was originally fired into the air, but its trajectory was deflected in mid-air by colliding with a stone thrown by a demonstrator.

2   This is a reference to the fire extinguisher Carlo was holding above his head at the moment he was killed.

Vittorio Agnoletto is a former member of the WSF International Council and currently a European United Left MEP. He was one of the main spokespeople for the Genoa Social Forum, who on the night of Carlo Giuliani's killing went on national media calling for people to demonstrate the following day. There was huge pressure to call it off, but in the event, 300,000 people marched. www.vittorioagnoletto.it

politics and the future of the movement

Vittorio Agnoletto

The movement that—according to the media— was born at Seattle and Genoa is neither one of many movements within the superstructure, nor reducible to a simple explosion of youth rebelling against the old— or indeed any other passing media fad.

The reasons for our existence are rooted in solid structural foundations. Indeed, not only is the current model of development unable to guarantee a future to the six billion plus people who currently inhabit the planet, but it cannot even ensure living standards or privileges for us, the population of the rich north west of the hemisphere. In fact, the uncontested dominance of the logic of profit is daily destroying the environment in which we live, is grappling with limited resources, and is encountering growing resistance from those billions of invisibles who are considered obstacles and superfluous to its plans.

The consequences of such a situation can be easily

mapped out in our daily lives in this society: the numbers of unemployed and poor are increasing alongside a sense of personal and collective insecurity—the feeling is growing that we are living in a fortress where it is impossible to think about the future with any degree of serenity.

After building up our expectations for 20 years of a wonderful future for the whole of humankind, neo-liberal theories—after dominating our collective imagination with promises of a modernity which would have finally, as if by magic, provided the answer to all our hopes, to the extent of even theorising the end of history as a dialectical, conflictual and contradictory process—all of this has now reached a dead end.

Even before its specific and broader setbacks, such as at the Cancun summit in September 2003, neo-liberal globalisation revealed its own failure in its inability to put forward a universal theory. It was incapable of interpreting and absorbing humanity's collective aspirations, or at least those in North America, Western Europe, Oceania and Japan who, as they are the centre of the world market, are the only groups worthy of attention in the eyes of the supporters of neo-liberal globalisation.

The initial cultural and ideological wave that began in the 1980s, which then became an economic cycle, now clearly shows its insurmountable limits. The constant recourse to war and its theorisation as a daily instrument of domination and conservation of the status quo represents, also in the eyes of world public opinion, the extreme weakness of this system and the dead-end street down which humanity is heading.

This irreversible crisis has been accelerated by the cultural emergence of developments directly linked to the struggles and activities—created in every corner of the planet—of social movements. These activities can no longer be thought of as simple acts of resistance, given that they are increasingly taking on a wider scope and reaching new theoretical depths. Porto Alegre, Florence and Mumbai are the three most important (but by no means the only) open-air universities that the movement has created for itself. And from these universities what does not emerge is the mere restating of the ideologies that dominated the 20th century, or at least not in the form in which they influenced actual lived history, often with tragic consequences.

> **Social movements are increasingly taking on a wider scope and reaching new theoretical depths**

Today's movement does not have its own finished theories, it does not counterpose its own single worked-out and systematic vision of the world to that of neo-liberal thought, and it is not a bearer of one specific ideology. But on the other hand neither is it a fuzzy conglomeration of ideals, hopes and aspirations: our pluralism does not mean we are an amorphous mishmash of people who come together on a casual basis.

We could define what is emerging as a new humanism, something that is being built and is destined to remain an open system of beliefs, even though it is able to trace out sufficiently precise contours, and ones that can be collectively accepted. It is a system of beliefs rooted in great ideals but strongly grounded in concrete proposals, and capable of achieving greater and greater syntheses. Some of the great ideas which have their origins in 19th and 20th century cultural traditions—such as socialism, communism, christianity, environmentalism and feminism—are accompanying us in this journey, and these are often heretical or

Vittorio
Agnoletto

29

critical variations in terms of the official ideologies which have had an actual historical expression.

But it would be profoundly mistaken to reduce all of this to a kind of meeting place of minority ideas. This would be a simplification which does not help us to understand the originality of this new humanism, which undoubtedly embodies the intellectual high points reached by previous attempts at human liberation, but which is not limited to just a mere summation—on the contrary it proposes new models of universal thought.

The central core of this thinking is the centrality of indivisible 'pluriversal' rights—in other words not just the rights of citizenship, which emerged from the French Revolution, and which could be exercised only according to your place of birth; nor universal rights, which although recognised throughout the world, come from one single source—the West; nor human rights, so as to move beyond an anthropocentric approach, according to which the inanimate and animal worlds are merely resources to be exploited; so above all indivisible rights, invariable and not dependent upon other priorities—rights that cannot be partially dispensed with according to the historical period, geographical position or current political demands.

The stubborn search for unity and the radical social nature that have characterised the movement up to now are not the result of extremism or ideological rigidity—on the contrary their origin lies in looking at the world from a standpoint of indivisible pluriversal rights. The theory and practice that emerge from this put the movement into a position of implacable hostility towards any form of neo-liberal thought, whether this be under the diluted form of impracticable Third Ways, or any system of thought or control over society which places profit rather than people at its centre.

A different approach to politics has already been born from this new humanism, nourished by the pluralism of theory and practice that the movement has spread throughout the planet. Over time, and with the diverse characteristics of every country, such an approach will lead in the West to the consolidation of an anti neo-liberal left current, able to cohere and respect the identities of organisational forms which already exist today. It will also be able to innovate organisational forms of representation according to is own practice of pluralism, diffused leadership and search for unity which continue to characterise the development of the movement itself. The movement will continue to have its own role, avoiding short-circuiting or any dangerous transformation into a party, something that has been attempted before without any great success. Far from developing indifference towards institutional politics, however, the movement can perform the role of a midwife in the birth of an anti neo-liberal left capable of confronting the future positively.

Vittorio
Agnoletto

Billy Hayes is the General Secretary of the Communication Workers Union (UK), which has nearly 300,000 members in telecommunications and IT. www.billyhayes.co.uk

the whole world over

Billy Hayes

At Seattle, in December 1999, substantial numbers of North American trade unionists joined the anti-globalisation movement in protest against the World Trade Organisation talks.

That action opened a new chapter in progressive politics. Of course, trade unions had taken an interest in the international trade issues for many years previously. Equally, many trade unionists had taken part in campaigns such as Jubilee 2000 on issues of Third World debt.

But the involvement of the unions at Seattle was new because the alliance between trade unions and anti-globalisation activists was there for the whole world to see—a massive action of forces from different traditions, sharing a common necessity.

There are those who, inside and outside the trade unions, deplore this alliance. However, I believe it is crucial to engage with the anti-globalisation movement.

The Communication Workers Union is supporting the European Social Forum in London, just as we have supported previous ESFs and the World Social Forum in Mumbai.

We have supported these initiatives because we believe it is in the direct and abiding interests of the working class to do so. As union activists we need to connect our union to the most advanced experiences of struggle, both national and international. It is the only way we can seriously address the problems we face.

Workers are being bombarded with propaganda about the benefits of globalisation. At its heart is the suggestion that anyone who opposes the unhindered movement of capital is living in another era. What this story lacks in coherence it makes up for in volume. It is almost the new 'common sense' that the world is converging around the benefits of free, deregulated, markets.

Only this is not true. And, because it's not true, the unions need to develop policies and alliances to counter the myths. For the truth is that the process of 'globalisation' is a process of more direct and accelerated exploitation.

So to deal with the myths we must analyse what is going on. The biggest myth of all is that globalisation is an economic success. The simple facts are that since the supposed start of this process the growth in the world economy has slowed and, by some measures, reduced.

Using IMF figures, the advanced countries in the world in 1970 received 68 percent of the world's income while embracing 20 percent of the world's population. By 2000, two decades after the neo-liberal consensus prevailed, these figures were that the advanced countries received 81 percent of the world's income, embracing 16 percent of the world's population.

Such a divergence can only be called a success if you are representing the interests of a minority of the peoples of the world. Yet the claim is that globalisation represents a benefit for all.

It may be argued that globalisation has increased the total product of the world to such an extent that, even with greater differentiation, everyone receives some benefit. This is not factually true either. Again, using IMF figures, in 1988 the GDP of the world, in constant 1995 dollars, was $4,885 per capita. In 2002 this figure was $4,778. Globalisation has reduced, not increased, the world's growth.

> In 1988 the GDP of the world was $4,885 per capita. In 2002 this figure was $4,778

Such facts need to be clearly promoted in the formulation of an alternative policy. A report has been recently published by the World Commission on the Social Dimension of Globalisation, called 'A Fair Globalisation: Creating Opportunities for All'. The Commission has a highly sympathetic view of globalisation, but even they sadly note, '…it is striking that since 1990 global GDP growth has been slower than in previous decades, the period in which globalisation has been most pronounced. At the very least this outcome is at variance with the more optimistic predictions on the growth-enhancing impact of globalisation'.

However we address the debates on sustainable resources and ecological protection, we must address the fact that the world's poor require growth in the economy to lift them out of poverty. Above all a growth in paid employment offers a route out of poverty.

Yet the facts are that unemployment is rising

uninterruptedly. According to the International Labour Organisation, 160 million people were unemployed at year end of 1997. By year end of 2003 this figure had reached 185.9 million. As globalisation is being more broadly promoted, so unemployment is rising.

Indeed, the general figures for poverty are completely clear. More people are becoming poor under globalisation. According to the World Bank the number of people living on less than a dollar a day was 1,237 million in 1990. This figure dropped to 1,100 million in 2000—apparently a success for globalisation. But in this decade 157 million Chinese were lifted out of poverty by China's growth. The Chinese economy is not part of the capitalist world economy, even after its reforms. By removing China from the statistics it is absolutely clear that in the capitalist markets there are more people in poverty in 2000 than in 1990.

Such debates may seem to be solely about the developing countries—this is not true of course.

Recently I attended the annual conference of the American Postal Workers Union. It was inspiring to witness the activity of trade unionists in George Bush's backyard. This is one of many incongruities that struck me forcibly during my visit.

Here is a nation of energetic, innovative and attractive people, led by a clique of nasty plutocrats. This is the richest nation on earth. Yet the 2004 annual census report reveals that in 2003 about 36 million Americans were living in poverty. Nearly 45 million people were without health coverage, representing nearly 15.6 percent of the population. 12.9 million children in the USA were living in poverty. Nearly a quarter of Afro-Americans were living below the poverty line. And all these figures have been getting worse under Bush.

If these are the contradictions of globalisation in the world's richest nation, how stark is the impact in the poorer nations?

Nor is the position in Britain today any better. According to the government's own figures, 14 million Britons are living in poverty. A recent report from End Child Poverty found that 3.8 million children in Britain were living in poverty.

According to the government's own figures, 14 million Britons are living in poverty

Such failures in the heartlands of the neo-liberal experiment give the lie to the idea that globalisation is resulting in a richer, fairer world.

So if another world is possible, it's because social forces representing a majority of people in the world can be drawn around common policies. The ESF and WSF are stepping stones to achieving such unity.

We must press our government on these questions. Unfortunately they still seem to be falling behind events. The Department for International Development recently issued a report called 'Labour Standards and Poverty Reduction'. It's rather more full of good intentions than good policies. At one point we read that 'action to promote workers' rights must be careful not to restrict the livelihood opportunities of poor people in development countries by pricing them out of jobs, whether in firms producing for foreign markets or for the home market, nor by intentional or unintentional protectionism in developed countries.'

The idea that poor people price themselves out of a job suggests no understanding of the actual position of the world's poor. Equally, it's unacceptable to imply the defence of employment in developed countries is dangerous to the economy.

Billy Hayes

In a document that is trying hard to help, such twitches show how deeply neo-liberal dogmas have infected political debate.

If governments want to help, they must direct more development capital towards the developing countries. The sad fact is, according to the OECD, Official Development Assistance (ODA) by the advanced countries is lower in 2002 than in 1970. Gordon Brown's commitment to move this towards 0.7 percent of gross national income is welcome, as is the commitment to the Millennium Development Goals. But let us not kid ourselves, we need to see very substantial flows of capital in the form of modern means of production to the developing countries. The idea that the poor should continue to produce basic commodities is a recipe for continual disadvantage to the developing countries.

Where is such capital to come from? A major contribution would be to end capital flows from developing countries to the advanced countries. Cancellation of the debt is crucial. Equally, the debate around the Tobin tax offers an opening for future policy. And let us not overlook the benefits accruing to the world if we achieve an end to imperialist wars. The World Commission on Social Dimension of Globalisation reports, rather wistfully, 'It would of course be both possible and desirable to generate resources through reallocation of military expenditures to development in both industrialised and developing countries. Total world military spending for 2001 has been estimated at US $839 billion. If the 15 largest military spenders agreed to divert just 5 percent to ODA, this would generate US $30 billion a year. This would surely make a greater contribution to global peace and security than it does through military expenditure.'

Yes, it surely would. Clearly this alone is a huge incentive to continue to build the anti-war movement.

As the largest voluntary organisations in the world, with over 164 million members, the trade unions must contribute to the debate. This will directly benefit their members, but will also substantially aid the world's poor.

With acknowledgement to Stephen Bell. I would like to thank Alan Freeman for allowing me to use material from the forthcoming book from Pluto Press, **The Politics of Empire and the Crisis of Globalisation**, edited by Alan Freeman and Boris Kagarlitsky.

❍ A copy of this article also appears on my personal weblog: www.billyhayes.co.uk

Billy Hayes

Susan George is Associate Director of the Transnational Institute in Amsterdam, a fellowship of scholars around the world whose work is intended to contribute to social justice. She is also Vice-President of ATTAC France (Association for Taxation of Financial Transaction to Aid Citizens). Her most recent books are **Another World is Possible If...** (2004) and **The Lugano Report: On Preserving Capitalism in the 21st Century** (1999). www.tni.org/george

taking the movement forward

Susan George

Bookmarks are publishing this collective volume to coincide with the European Social Forum of 2004 in London and they are right to set us this subject. It's the only one worth discussing because 'taking the movement forward' simultaneously means 'pushing our adversaries backward' until they fall over the edge of the cliff. Since I've recently had the opportunity to give my views elsewhere[1] on the global justice movement and to hold forth at some length on what to do and how to do it, let me concentrate here on four points which seem to me vital for the continuing success of the movement. For mnemonic convenience they all begin with 'PR' but have nothing to do with Public Relations: they are PRogrammes, PRiorities and PRagmatism, ending with a warning about PRecautions. These categories are intermingled but I will try to separate them a little, at least at the beginning.

Let me first take the notion of 'programme' in the narrow sense of the set of activities that take place during our Social Forums. These forums are high points of the movement year and ought to reflect both our evolution and the best we are capable of. I was heartened to learn that the 2005 World Social Forum in Porto Alegre will dispense with plenary sessions altogether in order to concentrate on seminars and workshops as these have the best chance to 'take the movement forward'. I was disappointed, on the other hand, that the 2004 European Social Forum in London still clings to the supposed necessity of plenaries even though there will be fewer than in previous years. Sorting out who gets to speak on what platform on what subject and with whom; how many speakers are allotted to each country and to each organisation; mixing them carefully according to gender, hue, hemispheric origin and I suppose religious profession, sexual orientation, height, weight and God knows what else; requiring each year long and multiple meetings all over Europe—all this has proven, as far as I can tell, a colossal waste of everyone's time and money. Let's get serious, people.

Social forums have the great advantage of bringing together many forces in a given country not necessarily used to working together and obliging them to do so, for a common cause. Perhaps some of these individuals or some of these organisations are still immature (vain?) enough to require the kind of public exposure and approbation that plenary sessions can convey (and, as an invited guest of the London ESF organising committee, I will myself perform if required to do so) but star turns are no longer what we need if indeed they ever were.

The same goes for restating the obvious and for

finger-pointing in the general direction of the usual suspects. Our topics are becoming over-ritualised—war and peace, democracy and fundamental rights, poverty and inequality and so on. It's pretty clear that as decent folk we favour some of these and deplore others. It's also safe to say, I think, that we already know pretty much what's wrong with the world and who or what is to blame. What, pray, is there left to say about the horrors of hunger, the devastation of debt, the iniquities of imperialism, the wickedness of war—and about all our other favourite subjects to which our responses are becoming not just predictable but positively Pavlovian.

It's time to define a minimum, common programme every activist in the world can agree on

If people, even quite young and/or inexperienced people, really don't know anything at all about these issues, which I seriously doubt, we can and should give them reading lists and set up courses and summer universities for them, but in future Social Forums I would hope we could stop the silly jockeying for speech slots, refrain from endless repetition and ceremonial condemnation, determine what issues we really need to talk about, get organised beforehand to do so, then hit the ground running.

I'm also surprised and distressed to note that the programmes of Social Forums tend not to focus on the truly key issue: power. If we're going to have all these plenary sessions, they should at least be geared to providing the audience with fresh insights into what the powerful have in store for us if we're not quick and smart enough to thwart and outwit them. We need to recognise the hard truth that they are much better organised than we are, at both the European and international levels. They've got the European Commission

Susan George

43

and UNICE (the European employers' union); the whole United States government, the Transatlantic Business Dialogue and the Paris and London Clubs (dealing with public and private Third World debt); the TNC's tax-dodges and mega-mergers; financial market freedom; the WTO and the GATS—you get my drift. What sorts of effective ripostes are we developing in our Social Forums to meet these challenges? Well, yes, we do regularly condemn war, poverty, human rights violations, obscene profits, etc, accompanied by soaring rhetoric. I'm sure that's got our adversaries positively trembling in their hand-made boots...

I know I'm being too harsh. Some valuable ideas are bound to emerge from the plenary sessions at the European and other Social Forums and these forums are indispensable for bringing together social and political forces in the service of a shared ideal. But I just wish for once we could use our time together in European Social Forums to decide, as Europeans, what we are going to do about, say, the Bolkestein Directive—and if you don't know what that is, it's because the movement isn't doing a good enough job of educating and organising. This EU Directive (which I hope may have been killed by the time you read this) is another little reward for our service corporations. If successfully implemented, the Bolkestein Directive would introduce a new legal principle and allow firms to apply the social and labour laws of the 'country of origin' to workers in all the European countries where the firms might happen to do business. A European (French, German, British, etc) company could set up its corporate headquarters in, say, Slovenia or Malta and its workers all over Europe would then have the great good fortune to receive Slovenian or Maltese wages and benefits.

My postulate about forums is that travelling somewhere for three or four days ought to be intellectually and politically profitable both to the person making the investment and to the movement itself. If this statement is valid, then it should logically follow that our time would be best spent in seminars and workshops genuinely oriented towards gaining the closest possible knowledge of our adversaries and to defining the collective strategies and actions most likely to make their lives miserable. As an out of fashion 19th century political philosopher might have said, 'We have identified and interpreted the targets: the point, however, is to hit them.'

Now let me combine the notions of PRogramme and PRiorities. In my view, if we are to take the global justice movement forward, it's time to define a minimum, common programme every activist in the world (or, when relevant, in Europe or another region) can agree on and in whose service political campaigning can be undertaken and pressure applied, right now. We need agreed-upon targets in the power structures both at European and world levels. Many activists already recognise the need for such a common programme whereas others claim it would condemn us to uniformity and consequent sterility. I disagree. Different people in different places would quite naturally continue to carry out their local and national struggles. But so long as our movement is about fighting neo-liberal globalisation and its destructive effects, it's almost tautological to state that we must determine what kind of globalisation we want instead and make clear what we are going to fight against and fight for. Otherwise, why should anyone bother listening to us, much less joining us?

As for Europe, I believe that if we want to save what's left of our public services and of the European social model, we've got to go after Bolke/Frankenstein-like measures and the GATS. The welfare state, although never perfectly achieved anywhere, is one of the greatest conquests of human history. It could serve as a beacon for the entire world. Why shouldn't all citizens of all countries enjoy rights—not charity but rights—including the right to work and to decent compensation if unemployed, to leisure and family time, to free education at all levels, to culture and to health care; to efficient public services and to the rule of law? Merely to list these is to show why the capitalist project must strike them down.

I'm quite willing to discuss other priorities. Global ills require global remedies and only international campaigning led by the international movement can provide the power to impose them. Our adversaries are all too often global in scope too and, once more, they act coherently, whereas we generally do not. The World Bank, the IMF and the WTO have a universal strategy; so do transnational corporations and banks (at least taken individually); even the Davos World Economic Forum, though made up of many disparate individuals, marches to the beat of the same neo-liberal drummer. How can the movement possibly score points off such powerful institutions if it remains dispersed, working on a thousand different issues, never really uniting in a single struggle around any of them?

One of the most effective actions in decades was the worldwide protest on 15 February 2003 against the American war in Iraq. Possibly because we weren't actually able to stop the war (no one could have done that), people may have classed the day as a 'failure' and not reflected enough on its huge significance—15 February was in fact a historic first. During the Vietnam War, thanks to arduous months of planning and expensive transatlantic phone calls, it was occasionally possible to stage simultaneous demos in Europe and the US, but never anything on the scale of 15 February. In 2003 it wasn't just Europeans and North Americans, but Latin Americans, Africans, Asians, Australians, citizens of many Muslim countries—every continent was involved, including Antarctica, where a scientific mission took part. This unified, organised outpouring of protest caused a reluctant *New York Times* to refer to the peace movement as 'the second superpower', even if that statement (like much else of what one can read in the *New York Times*) turned out to be not quite true. We must now try to mobilise the same kind of strength and unity in the name of global justice and put them on the front page.

However, even assuming people can grasp the truth of that old cliché 'In unity lies strength', we must still carefully define our priorities: we cannot have an international programme that looks like a laundry list. However convinced each movement activist may be that his or her own pet issue is the most important one in the known universe, we've still got to think more about what's do-able together now that we finally have a worldwide movement; in other words, we have to proceed with PRagmatism. This means thinking about how we might start winning instead of scattering our human and material resources all over the landscape.

Pragmatism begins with asking, and answering, relevant questions: Where is the adversary weakest, intellectually, morally and politically? Which of our campaigns are most likely to touch raw and exposed

Establishment nerves? Where are the contradictions of the global capitalist system sharpest? On what issues could we recruit the most allies? Which demands would provoke the least scope for media hostility? What victory, if achieved, would provide the greatest good for the greatest number and be the best launching pad for future campaigns?

Shouldn't it be possible, with five years worth of experience under our belts since Seattle, to settle on one, at most two, initial issues that play to our strong points and take advantage of their weak ones, and then campaign on them, all together? I'm not sure the movement is yet mature enough to do this, but I am certain we must at least try to find out whether it is or not. If we find that it is, then we should decide on a couple of concrete objectives people either all over Europe or all over the world can cooperate on, objectives they want to turn into reality.

Let's face it: despite a few minor and mostly temporary setbacks, our adversaries are still very much in the saddle. We badly need a victory, if possible a large, visible victory, one that pushes them a little closer to the cliff's edge.

Let me repeat: such a conscious choice wouldn't mean abandoning all our other ongoing campaigns— simply that everyone understands that when there's an action push to be carried out and demos to be planned, officials to be besieged and governments harassed, then those activities really are priorities for everyone at that particular time. For such an endeavour to work, we would need some sort of elected international steering committee. Couldn't we try to develop such an idea at the coming Social Forums on different continents, call for candidates, organise an election system and secure a budget? Naturally no one can guarantee that a more sharply focused strategic choice would bring us victory but it seems clear that our adversaries savour every moment we remain dispersed and, for most practical purposes, off their backs.

My own basket of global campaigning priorities among which we might choose would include debt cancellation, international taxation with democratic redistribution in order to move towards welfare states everywhere, global warming and ecological destruction, food security and sovereignty, the protection and improvement of public services (including ousting GATS), total overhaul of the international financial institutions and the establishment of an International Trade Organisation along the lines proposed by John Maynard Keynes 60 years ago. We also desperately need to confront the power and influence of the United States of America, no matter who may be the next president. For the sake of PRagmatism, I'd be happy to narrow down all these worthy subjects to one or two global PRiorities and would hope others could also show flexibility.

For example, debt might well be the best target, politically and strategically speaking. Before the Jubilee 2000 campaign needlessly self-destructed (in my view one of the worst strategic mistakes in recent history) it had become clear that politicians were under pressure and on the way to being forced to act. Now the heat is off and the debtors are still in bondage. In this connection, I think we as a movement must also ask pointed questions of some of the larger and more powerful NGOs which seem to think their supporters are so bored and fickle that they must

One of the most effective actions in decades was the worldwide protest on 15 February 2003

Susan George

49

change campaigns every couple of years or risk seeing their resources dry up. I can't see why else they would have abandoned debt at precisely the moment governments and the International Financial Institutions were being forced to make their first concessions and major cancellation promises—which they predictably and promptly broke as soon as they could get away with it. Meanwhile, Sub-Saharan Africa is still paying out $28,000 every minute in debt service. One could equip a fair number of schools and clinics with all that loose change.

Debt (and its accompanying structural adjustment programmes) would have a lot of advantages as a campaign objective: it is certainly one of the most important contributing factors to hunger, collapsed health, water and education systems, plummeting commodity prices, the switch from public services to private corporate control, the freedom of capital movements and in a general way, to huge leverage for the North over the whole range of Southern policy choices. As a system of domination, debt is far more intelligent than colonialism, requiring no police, army or expatriate administration and even regularly bringing in a bit of revenue. Debt cancellation could be linked to a system requiring that the savings be spent on the priorities determined by the people of the country concerned (what I call 'democratic conditionality').

Although personally I worked on debt for over a decade beginning in about 1984, I now devote little time to the subject and am more concerned with the WTO, especially the GATS, and to a lesser degree GMOs. But I'd be quite prepared to hold high the banner for debt cancellation once more if the whole movement were to agree on the objective, a strategy and a timetable. Or someone else can make a case for another subject—heaven knows action against global warming is urgent. But whatever it is, let's make up our minds, choose a clear priority and get moving.

Let me now come to another PR word: PRecaution. In order to take the movement forward, let's not get side-tracked or bogged down with huge, unwieldy abstractions like 'defeating the market' or 'overthrowing capitalism'. Any priority we choose, if we win, is necessarily going to lessen both the power of the market and of the neo-liberal capitalist system. I'm not romantic (or foolhardy?) enough to believe that capitalism can be brought down at a stroke. There's no Winter Palace and consequently it cannot be stormed. A few days after 11 September, Wall Street was up and running again.

So if we were to win on, say, debt, it would of course be only a partial victory, but it would be won against the banks still receiving comfortable interest payments, against the corporations eager for further privatisation opportunities; against the IMF, the World Bank and their cohorts of structural adjusters; against Northern governments, particularly the US; against the Washington consensus. It would be a victory for the South and, if the democratic conditionality issue were properly dealt with, for the people of the now indebted countries who would finally have the right to choose their own priorities and control where the money was going.

In conclusion, let me add a final precautionary note: I lived through another movement, against the Vietnam War and all the evils it arose from. We tried to fight racism and sexism and move towards peace, decolonisation and social justice. And then, sometime in the early to mid-1970s, the movement petered out.

The 'hippies' trailed off to wherever it is hippies trail off to (many joining advertising agencies or banks) and it became clear that their goal all along had been the same as that of the majority, that is, individual gratification and private consumption, albeit consumption of different things. The hard-built structures of the anti-war movement collapsed. And then suddenly, there were Maggie and Ronnie in Downing Street and the White House. The rest is history—the quite nasty history we've now got to deal with.

No one knows exactly why movements emerge but it's certain they are fragile, evanescent and can disappear as mysteriously as they appeared. I would suggest that the major causes of their demise are boredom, discouragement and self-indulgence. People get bored and discouraged if they never win. Self-indulgence isn't necessarily just the hippie kind (let me smoke my grass and to hell with the world). It could also mean in the 21st century refusing to put aside one's own preferred cause, no matter how worthy, for even a short time in favour of working with others on a winnable worldwide campaign.

But I am hopeful. The movement is made up of remarkable people with enormous talent, knowledge and stamina. If collectively we are smart enough, mature enough, determined enough to prefer winning to mere self-indulgence, we've got a chance. And that, to introduce a final PR word, would be profound PRogress.

Note

1 Susan George, **Another World is Possible If...** Verso, London and New York, 2004

Naomi Klein is an award-winning journalist and author of the international best-seller **No Logo** (2000). She writes for numerous publications including the **Guardian**, the **New Statesman**, **Newsweek International**, the **New York Times**, the **Village Voice** and **Ms. Magazine**, and has regular columns in the **Globe and Mail** newspaper (Canada) and the **Nation** magazine (US). A collection of her work is available in **Fences and Windows: Dispatches from the Front Lines of the Globalisation Debate** (2002). Naomi recently co-produced a documentary with Avi Leavis about resistance in Argentina called **The Take**. www.nologo.org

join the global mutiny

Naomi Klein

Five days after Bush landed on that infamous aircraft carrier and declared, 'Mission accomplished,' he unveiled the real mission behind the war: there would be a free trade zone covering the entire Middle East in the next ten years, NAFTA for the Arab world. This is the true Bush doctrine: bomb first, buy later— shock therapy through shock and awe military force.

That is, and always has been, the true mission in Iraq, and it must never be accomplished.

Those of us who have spent time in Iraq in recent months know that this mission is on the verge of collapse. And collapse it must because what is unfolding in Iraq is neo-liberalism at its most brutish and obscene. Our job—all of us who opposed this war and who oppose neo-liberalism as a never-ending war—is to do our best to help that collapse along.

The Iraq mission isn't just failing because of the staggering incompetence and crushing hypocrisy of the US occupation. It's also failing because the occupation has encountered wave after wave of tenacious, courageous resistance, not only by armed Iraqi fighters, but other kinds of resistance as well.

Months of inflammatory US aggression in Iraq has inspired what can only be described as a mutiny: thousands of soldiers, workers and politicians under the command of the US occupation authority are suddenly refusing to follow orders and abandoning their posts. First Spain announced it would withdraw its troops, then Honduras, the Dominican Republic, Nicaragua and Kazakhstan. South Korean and Bulgarian troops were pulled back to their bases, while New Zealand may withdraw its engineers. El Salvador, Norway, the Netherlands and Thailand will likely be next.

Then there is the mutiny within the Iraqi army, a security forced created and controlled by the US military. Since April, Iraqi soldiers have been in open revolt, donating their weapons to resistance fighters in the south and refusing to fight in Falluja, saying that they didn't join the army to kill other Iraqis. Major General Martin Dempsey, commander of the 1st Armoured Division, admits that 'about 40 percent [of Iraqi security officers] walked off the job because of intimidation. And about 10 percent actually worked against us.'

And it's not just Iraq's soldiers who have been deserting the occupation. Four ministers of the Iraqi Governing Council have resigned their posts in protest. Remember, these are the people who got their jobs because they were thought to be willing puppets of the US occupation—but now even the puppets are refusing to perform. In addition, more than half the Iraqis with jobs in the secured 'green zone'—as translators, drivers, cleaners—are not showing up for work.

And Al-Sabah, the psyops newspaper created by the US military, lost its entire staff in May after they walked off the job in protest against editorial interference. You know your occupation is in trouble when even the propagandists turn on you.

Minor mutinous signs are emerging even within the ranks of the US military: Privates Jeremy Hinzman and Brandon Hughey have applied for refugee status in Canada as conscientious objectors and Staff Sergeant Camilo Mejia is facing court martial after he refused to return to Iraq on the grounds that he no longer knew what the war was about. Higher ranking officers have echoed the sentiment. Army Colonel Paul Hugues, who helped formulate policy for the war, told the Washington Post in May that 'we don't understand the war we're in'. And let's not forget that it was a US soldier who first blew the whistle on torture at the Abu Ghraib prison, an unsung act of courage with world-changing consequences.

> **Minor mutinous signs are emerging even within the ranks of the US military**

Rebelling against the US authority in Iraq is neither treachery, nor is it giving 'false comfort to terrorists', as Bush claimed when he scolded Spain's new prime minister. It is an entirely rational and principled response to policies that have put everyone living and working under US command in grave and unacceptable danger. When the commander has lost it, mutiny is the only sane response. This is a view shared by 52 former British diplomats, who in April sent a letter to prime minister Tony Blair stating, 'There is no case for supporting policies which are doomed to failure.'

And the US occupation of Iraq does appear doomed on all fronts: military, political and economic.

Naomi Klein

The military front

We see the gruesome evidence of military failure every day: a dramatically rising death toll, both among Iraqis and occupation forces; war crimes committed not just in the prisons but in the streets of Fallujah, Sadr City, and Najaf. In only a few short weeks this spring the US managed to turn a resistance movement that began with small numbers of Saddam loyalists operating in the shadows into something akin to an Iraqi intifada. The war against the occupation is now being fought out in the open by regular people defending their homes and neighbourhoods. In addition to swelling the ranks of the resistance, the US has also managed to unite its enemies. When simultaneous assaults were launched on Falluja and Najaf in April, Sunnis and Shias both were both forced to bury their children and witness the desecration of their holy sites. Many responded to this shared tragedy by burying ancient rivalries and joining forces. Instead of the civil war between Sunnis and Shias that Washington has been predicting, the US inadvertently created a united front—united against the occupation.

The political front

The idea that the United States intends to bring real democracy to Iraq is now irredeemably discredited, even in the eyes of Iraqis who dared to hope that the freedom they longed for under dictatorship could flow from this war. They may be overjoyed to be rid of Saddam Hussein, but nobody is waiting for US tanks to deliver democracy any more. Too many relatives of Iraqi Governing Council members have landed plum jobs and rigged contracts, too many groups demanding direct elections have been fired upon, too many newspapers have been closed down, too many mosques have been destroyed and too many Arab journalists have been murdered while trying to do their jobs.

The economic front

White House plans to turn Iraq into a model free market economy are in equally rough shape, plagued by corruption scandals and the rage of Iraqis who have seen few benefits—either in services or jobs—from the reconstruction. Corporate trade shows have been cancelled across country, investors are relocating to Amman and Iraq's housing minister estimates that more than 1,500 foreign contractors have fled the country to avoid the violence and kidnappings. Bechtel, meanwhile, admits that it can no longer operate 'in the hot spots' (and there are precious few cold ones); truck drivers are afraid to travel the roads with valuable goods; and General Electric has suspended work on key power stations. The only private companies doing any serious work in Iraq are the security firms, renting out tens of thousands of highly paid mercenary soldiers and prison guards. Reconstruction may be stalled, but the destruction business is still booming.

Naomi Klein

Taken together, the crisis facing the US in Iraq is nearly complete: its 'liberating' soldiers are despised as occupiers, its politicians are viewed as thieves, and its businesses can neither buy nor rebuild. But a US failure is not the same as a victory for the people of Iraq—anything could fill the vacuum that is being created, from oppressive religious fundamentalism to US-installed dictatorship, to decades of civil warfare. Besides, the ideologues who waged this war have not given up—if anything, they have become more desperate to win, more bloodily determined to extract the spoils of their war, whatever the cost.

So this isn't a moment for the anti-war movement

to be satisfied with self-congratulation and I told you so's—that's not good enough. Rather—we have to use this window of weakness to make our demands for meaningful change in Iraq—and we have to make them with even more clarity and forcefulness than that with which we opposed the war. Because we opposed the invasion of Iraq not out of any love for Saddam, but because, behind the rhetoric of "liberation," many of us detected the most savage and ambitious expression of imperialism in recent history. Now that this project is collapsing, we owe it to the people of Iraq, who have suffered so long under dictatorship, war, sanctions and now occupation, to do everything we can to help them achieve their goal of real freedom and self-determination.

But how do we do that? Easy: we listen to the voices on the streets of Baghdad, Basra, Najaf and Falluja. Even in the midst of enormous daily suffering and unimaginable insecurities, Iraqis have made their desires for genuine sovereignty abundantly clear. Hundreds of thousands have taken to the streets chanting 'Yes, yes election, no, no selections.' There is also widespread rejection of the interim constitution, written by US occupation chief Paul Bremer and his appointees on the Iraqi Governing Council. The document is seen as a thinly veiled attempt by the US to continue to control Iraq's future long after Iraqi 'sovereignty' has been declared. It contains a clause that states, 'The laws, regulations, orders, and directives issued by the Coalition Provisional Authority…shall remain in force' under Iraq's 'sovereign' government. These laws include Bremer's Order 39, which drastically changed Iraq's previous constitution to allow foreign companies to own 100 percent of Iraqi assets, and to take 100 percent of their profits out of the country. In other words, the constitution makes it illegal for Iraqis to change the laws written by their occupiers.

Yet Iraqis have made it clear that they oppose the privatisation of the oil industry and of state companies because they fear more layoffs in a country where unemployment is already around 60 percent. They also oppose US plans to continue to control billions of dollars in reconstruction funds, which they rightly see as their money—not Bechtel's or Halliburton's. Again and again Iraqis have told politicians, journalists, pollsters and religious leaders that they want to rebuild their ravaged country themselves, using their knowledge, experience and their own people.

But by far the clearest demand is for the occupation of Iraq to end.

So far the Bush regime has proven deaf to these demands coming from the Iraqi people. The hated constitution stands, elections have been postponed, and US engineers have begun construction on 14 'enduring bases' in Iraq, capable of housing the 110,000 soldiers posted for at least two more years—which is why it's our job to bring these demands from the occupied streets of Baghdad to the ears of the decision makes in Washington. And the demands are clear:

Troops out now

Many argue that if the US were to withdraw, the country would descend into chaos. John Kerry believes more troops are needed, to provide security for the transition process. But US troops provide security to no one—not to the Iraqis, not to their fellow soldiers, not to the UN. American soldiers have become a direct provocation to more violence, not only because of the brutality of the occupation in Iraq but also because of US support for Israel's deadly occupation of Palestinian territory. In the minds of many Iraqis, the two occupations have blended into a single anti-Arab outrage, with Israeli and US soldiers viewed as interchangeable and Iraqis openly identifying with Palestinians.

Without US troops, the major incitement to violence would be removed, allowing the country to be stabilised with far fewer soldiers. Iraq would still face security challenges—there would still be extremists willing to die to impose Islamic law, as well as attempts by Saddam loyalists to regain power. On the other hand, with Sunnis and Shiites now united against the occupation, it's the best possible moment for an honest broker to negotiate an equitable power-sharing agreement.

With that in mind, combat troops who participated in the invasion and occupation could be replaced with genuine peacekeepers, made up of Iraqis from every part of the country, and from neighbouring Arab states. But what cannot be allowed to happen is a rebranded occupation under the UN flag. To prevent this, any stabilising force in Iraq must have two jobs and two jobs only. First, it must secure the country for immediate elections so that Iraqis can directly choose their own government. Second, it must ensure that by the time Iraqis get to the polls, there is still something left to vote for. That means fiercely fending off all attempts to shackle the future government of Iraq to the US military and economic agenda. So…

Ditch the interim constitution

The document is a blueprint for outsourcing the occupation. It is illegal, illegitimate and must be discarded. Some argue that it is needed to prevent open elections from delivering the country to religious extremists. Yet according to a February 2004 poll by Oxford Research

International, Iraqis have no desire to see their country turned into another Iran. Asked to rate their favoured political system and actors, 48.5 percent of Iraqis ranked a 'democracy' as most important, while an 'Islamic state' received 20.5 percent support. If Iraqis are given the chance to vote their will, there is every reason to expect that the results will reflect a balance between their faith and their secular aspirations.

Put the money in trust

A crucial plank of any transition to real sovereignty is safeguarding Iraq's national assets: its oil revenue, the remaining oil for food programme money (currently administered by the United States with no oversight), as well as what's left of the $18.4 billion in reconstruction funds still being controlled by the US. All of it must be put in trust, to be spent by an elected Iraqi government. And it's not enough for the troops to go home: Halliburton, Bechtel, Shell and Dyncorp have to go home too.

No privatisation without representation

The laws Paul Bremer passed to allow Iraq to be sold off to foreign investors were illegal to start with and no future government of Iraq should be bound by them. But there are other, less visible ways that Washington is trying to force Iraq's next government to follow the neo-liberal rule book. It has already begun the process of getting membership for Iraq in the World Trade Organisation, and it has started negotiating the terms for an extensive loan package from the International Monetary Fund. Both these processes violate the most basic principles of national sovereignty and must be halted, leaving all decisions about Iraq's economic future to an elected government.

Full reparations now

Instead of the status quo of disguising robbery as reconstruction, Iraq must receive massive war reparations, to be administered by the people of Iraq as they choose. The sum must cover not only the rebuilding of bombed-out infrastructure, but also the humanitarian crisis created by war, sanctions and occupation. This level of financial compensation will give Iraqis something more important than money—it will give them the freedom not to sell off their national assets if they choose, as well as the freedom not to give up their sovereignty in exchange for an IMF or World Bank loan.

No matter how many times George Bush declares victory, a simple fact remains: this war isn't over yet. I won't say that we can win, because to speak of winning is to succumb to its barbaric logic. But there is something we can do: we can keep them from winning. We can make them lose—lose their power over Iraq, lose their military bases, lose their corrupt reconstruction contracts, lose their free trade zone, lose their dream of a privatised Iraq. And that would be a victory. Because the damage of this war cannot be undone. But at least the men who waged it can be taught that it doesn't pay to set our world on fire and try to turn a profit off the ashes.

This essay first appeared in **The Nation** magazine.

million march against war during the European Social Forum in Florence,
vember 2002 Picture: Jeff Brewster

Carlo Giuliani, 23, shot dead by Italian police at the G8 Summit, Genoa, July 20

3 million attend CGIL rally against Berlusconi and his plans for market labour reforms, Rome, Italy Picture: Jess Hurd www.reportdigial.co.uk

D14 demonstration for a different Europe during the EU Summit in Brussels,

Graffiti outside the UN building, Geneva, Switzerland, 2003
Picture: Noel Douglas

Gay and lesbian contingent on a demonstration against the IMF and World Bank, Prague, Czech Republic, September 2000 Picture: Jess Hurd www.reportdigital

Bolivian revolt, October 2003

World Social Forum in Porto Alegre, Brazil 2003

Piqueteros demonstration, Argentina, July 2004
Picture: Sebastian Hatcher

Protester hangs anti water privatisation banner from bridge in front of the Jet D'Eau fountain in Geneva, Switzerland, 2003. Picture: Jess Hurd www.reportdigital.co.uk

Indian Workers from the Forest Workers Union, at the World Social Forum in Mumbai, India, January 2004. Picture: Jess Hurd www.reportdigital.co.uk

Women collect rubbish for recycling during the World Social Forum, Mumbai, January 2004. Picture: Jess Hurd www.reportdigital.co.uk

STOP THE BLAIR RICH PROJE[CT]

tudents protest against top up fees outside parliament 2003
cture: Jess Hurd www.reportdigital.co.uk

2 million march in London on the historic 15 February global day of action against war, 2003 Picture: Jess Hurd www.repo tdigital.co.uk

Iraq and Vietnam Veterans Against the War and Military Families for Peace, Ne
York City, September 2004 Picture: Jess Hurd www.reportdigital.co.uk

500,000 march against the Republican national convention in New York city, August 2004 Picture: Jess Hurd www.reportdigital.co.uk

Alex Callinicos is a leading member of the Socialist Workers Party (UK). He teaches politics at the University of York. His most recent books are **The New Mandarins of American Power** (2004) and **An Anti-Capitalist Manifesto** (2003).

the future of the anti-capitalist movement

Alex Callinicos

The European Social Forum in London makes an important punctuation mark in the history of the movement against capitalist globalisation. It comes shortly before what amounts to the fifth anniversary of that movement's birth on 30 November 1999, the great day of protest at the World Trade Organisation summit in Seattle.[1] But any assessment of the subsequent development of the movement must connect Seattle with Genoa.

On 20-21 July 2001 police violence against protesters at the Group of Eight summit in Genoa climaxed in the shooting of a young demonstrator, Carlo Giuliani: in response 300,000 people from all over Europe took to the streets of the old port. The Genoa days may come to be seen as a turning point in the history of the European left. Far away the biggest confrontation to date between the anti-capitalist movement and the state, they marked the moment when this movement finally took root in Europe, and in a form significantly different from the North American networks involved in Seattle, given the high profile in the protests of the European radical left, most notably the Partito della Rifondazione Comunista (PRC). Moreover, the networks that mobilised for Genoa provided the impetus for the European Social Forum that first met, triumphantly, in Florence in November 2002.

The challenge of war

More immediately, Genoa's significance cannot be separated from what came less than two months later—the terrorist atrocities of 11 September 2001 and the proclamation by President George W Bush of a global, permanent 'war on terrorism'. Toni Negri has well brought out the connection between Genoa and 9/11:

What began as a demonstration against the eight major states became transformed into a demonstration against war—and this precisely at the moment when the G8 decided, in a sort of feverish anticipation of September 11, to add to the panoply of devices for controlling populations and movements the formidable instrument of war. There was therefore an anticipation on both sides, by both the G8 and the anti-global protesters. We found ourselves on the edge of war, and war did in fact come. [2]

And when the war came, it was networks that had mobilised for Genoa that played a central role in building powerful anti-war movements, most notably in Britain, Italy and Spain, the three European states most closely allied to the Bush administration. 9/11 thus had a contrasting effect on the two sides of the northern Atlantic: while it struck the anti-capitalist movement in the US a blow from which it has yet to recover, in Europe resistance to the 'war on terrorism' stimulated the further development of the movement. Moreover, out of the first ESF in Florence came the call to make 15 February 2003 first a European and then (after the call was taken up by the World Social Forum in Porto Alegre, Brazil, in January 2003) a global day of protest against the war in Iraq. A recent study by Dominique Reynié has documented both the scale of this anti-war movement and the fact that it was strongest in Europe: Reynié estimates that between 3 January and 12 April 2003, 35.5 million people took part in 2,978 demonstrations against war in Iraq. Of those demonstrators 20.3 million were in what would soon become the expanded European Union of 25 states, 57 percent of the total.[3]

By any standards, the construction of a global anti-war movement was a historic achievement. It is, however, no reason for complacency: after all, despite the protests, the United States and Britain invaded Iraq, which remains (notwithstanding the 'return of sovereignty' to a puppet government) under foreign occupation. Moreover, the anti-capitalist movement burst fully into the public arena in Seattle by challenging the entire logic of neo-liberal globalisation. Despite some tactical defeats in the leading capitalist states' attempts to force through further liberalisation of international trade—most notably the failure of the WTO summits in Seattle and in Cancún in September 2003—the neo-liberal economic agenda continues relentlessly to roll on, implemented domestically even by governments such as Lula's in Brazil that rhetorically denounce it.

Mention of Lula (whose now ruling Workers Party

was closely associated with the first three World Social Forums, which were held in Brazil in 2001-3) highlights an increasingly embarrassing problem—politics. The first wave of protests in 1999-2001—Seattle, Prague, Quebec City, Gothenburg, Genoa—were informed by a sense of euphoria: after what was supposed to have been the End of History, large numbers of people had taken to the streets to challenge the dominant neo-liberal ideology. Questions of the movement's own strategy and of the kind of alternatives we should be seeking didn't loom large.[4]

Moreover, many leading activists and intellectuals sought to keep these issues off the agenda. Various factors were involved here—the concern to maintain unity among very diverse networks and coalitions, a suspicion of traditional left wing politics that reflected negative experiences in the revolutionary, social democratic or Stalinist lefts, internalisation of the ideas of autonomous social movements as an alternative to political parties and of civil society as a sphere independent of the state and capital that came to flourish in the 1980s. Even figures on the more radical wing of the anti-capitalist movement would make the claim—itself profoundly ideological—that the movement is 'non-ideological'. The Charter of Principles of the World Social Forum conceives the WSF (and its more localised counterparts, which are required to conform to this Charter) as an 'open meeting place' that takes no decisions and formally bans political parties from participation.[5]

Such a cautious attitude may have made sense in the early phases of the movement, when the main impetus was simply to get people talking and working together and mutual confidence-building was an important priority. Today, however, particularly after the experiences of Genoa and the anti-war movement, the political issues facing activists have become much tougher. Partly in response, a process of political differentiation has occurred that has seen several distinct currents—one might even say parties—emerge.

In Europe three broad and internally heterogeneous tendencies stand out: a reformist right associated particularly with ATTAC (which campaigns against international financial speculation) in France that conceives the movement as a means of exerting pressure on nation-states to impose greater regulation on financial markets; a radical left—notably the PRC in Italy, the Ligue Communiste Révolutionnaire in France, and the Socialist Workers Party in Britain—that seeks to connect resistance to neo-liberalism with a broader project of social transformation; and autonomists—for example, the Italian disobbedienti—who use the Marxist vocabulary of Hardt's and Negri's *Empire* but tend to regard the anti-capitalist movement with its distinctive ways of organising as an end in itself through which the existing structures of power can be 'evaded' and new forms of life constructed.[6]

What is interesting is the extent to which reformists and autonomists, despite being poles apart in their rhetoric, converge on the issue that has underlain many of the strategic problems the movement has had to confront since 9/11—the state. The movement began, after all, as an anti-globalisation movement. In the dominant discourse of the 1990s, globalisation was equated with a decisive weakening of the nation-state. Both the reformist and the autonomist wings of the movement took this discourse as their starting point.

Between 3 January and 12 April 2003, 35.5 million people took part in 2,978 anti-war demos

Alex Callinicos

101

Both took for granted the decline of the nation-state, even if they attached different signs, respectively negative and positive, to this apparent fact. On the one hand, ATTAC conceived the Tobin tax on international capital movements as a way of rebuilding the economic power of the nation-state; on the other hand, *Empire* announced the emergence of a new form of transnational capitalist power marked by the disappearance of national sovereignty.

The epochal events of 2001 shattered the assumption common to these contrasting approaches: 'Genoa highlighted the role of organised state violence in defence of capitalist property relations. The war in Afghanistan then underlined the external dimension of state violence, as the enormous military strength of the Pentagon was deployed to reassert US hegemony.'[7] The nation-state was alive and well, and far from benign. Both reformists and autonomists responded by denying that there was any connection between neo-liberal globalisation and war.

Pierre Khalfa of ATTAC claims that 'liberal globalisation is characterised by the extreme liquidity of "countryless" capital and by a weakening of the links between the nation-state and the great "national" firms... Liberal globalisation probably doesn't need armed force to impose itself.'[8] Michael Hardt, co-author of *Empire*, argues even more strongly that imperialism and war were bad for business and that rational capitalists should support Empire as a pacific form of capitalist development.[9] On both wings of the movement there were similarly negative assessments of the way in which the anti-capitalist movement allowed itself to become 'diverted' into mobilising against the war in Iraq. Bernard Cassen, founder of ATTAC, complained about 'an obsession with war' at the first ESF in Florence.[10] Hardt wrote after 15 February 2003: 'It is unfortunate but inevitable that much of the energies that have been active in the globalisation protests have now at least temporarily redirected against the war.'[11]

Underlying these responses to the development of the anti-war movement was a shared theoretical misunderstanding, the failure to see that contemporary capitalism is still also imperialism, and thus is constituted by two distinct though interlocking forms of competition—the economic struggles among firms for markets and geopolitical rivalries between states.[12] But, at the same time, reformists and autonomists have divergent attitudes towards the state. Reformists want to use the state to humanise capitalism: George Monbiot has offered a particularly robust defence of this strategy, arguing for a 'global democratic revolution' that will create transnational political structures capable of restraining unbridled capitalism.[13] Autonomists, by contrast, seek to evade the problem of state power, an approach summed up by the self-refuting title of John Holloway's book, *Change the World without Taking Power*.

Alex Callinicos

103

But even here there can be a convergence between reformism and the autonomist rhetoric of 'anti-power'. Thus Khalfa writes:

Unlike past movements for emancipation, the movement for another globalisation doesn't seek power, it situates itself in the sphere of counter-powers. It has therefore been able to avoid a number of strategic debates, such as that on 'reform and revolution', that have profoundly divided movements for emancipation in the past. Hence the problem posed by the presence of parties, even leaving aside the orientations they can take, and the difficulty of thinking how to relate with them, and more generally with the political sphere, apart from adopting a stance of distrust. This distrust is all the more important since the movement for another world is obliged to rely on political parties with which it disagrees to implement its proposals.[14]

It is particularly interesting to see how talk of 'counter-power' and an affirmation of the exclusion of political parties leads here to a conception of the anti-capitalist movement as, in effect, a pressure group that seeks to extract reforms from the mainstream parties. The question of reform and revolution is 'avoided' simply by collapsing into reformism. But how does such a stance allow us to confront the political reality that all mainstream parties, including those of the social democratic left, support the neo-liberal agenda and implement it when in office? What does reformism mean in an era when not simply are there few new reforms, but old ones are being taken back thanks to privatisation, deregulation and reductions in social expenditure? This is the problem faced by mainstream social movements—not only the trade unions, but also the big non-governmental organisations that seek largely unavailingly to squeeze more enlightened policies from governments on which they are dependent for much of their funding.

The reformism of the ATTAC leadership is no mere intellectual stance: it has immediate political implications. Soon after the fall of Baghdad, Cassen wrote a paper in which he mused, 'How, in France, to support Chirac abroad while fighting Raffarin at home?' How, in other words, in opposing Bush's war drive to follow the leadership of a right wing government implementing neo-liberal policies at home? He goes on to wonder whether or not ATTAC should support the proposals for European defence put forward by France, Germany and Belgium. 'Confronted with an American strategy based on the discretionary use of force,' Cassen argues, 'the movement for another world can't practise an ostrich-like policy with regard to defence.'[15] The implication is plain: the anti-capitalist movement should be backing European imperialism as a counterweight to US imperialism.

Cassen's support for European militarism flows from his broader politics. If you believe that systemic transformation is impossible and that the best we can hope for is some more regulated version of capitalism, then you are likely to be sceptical about mass mobilisation as an answer to the military might of American imperialism. Given this perspective, it is entirely natural to seek a counterweight to the US within the existing system—and the obvious candidate for this role is the European Union. Only a revolutionary perspective that targets the entire imperialist system, not simply the most powerful actor in that system, provides a principled basis for resisting this logic. Far from being 'avoidable', the ancient dilemma of reform or revolution is inescapable.

The same kind of pressure group politics can be found on the autonomist wing of the movement as well. Hardt and Negri have called on the US to abandon trying unilaterally to dominate the world as a 'global monarch' and to 'collaborate with the other dominant nation states, the multinational corporations, and the supranational institutions that compose the global aristocracies'. They describe both neo-liberalism and the 'war on terrorism' as forms of 'unilateralism' that are contrary to the interests of global capitalism and suggest that the 'imperial aristocracies' should ally themselves with the 'most progressive governments of the global South [such as Brazil under Lula] and the globalisation protest movements' to 'orient their project of renewal of productive forces and energies in the global economic system'. This prudent advice to the powerful (published in the magazine of the World Economic Forum) differs little in substance from the critique of the Bush administration's unilateralism by ruling class figures such as Zbigniew Brzezinski, who argues that the US must ally itself with the EU in order stably to rule the world, and has warned of the political challenge that the anti-capitalist movement presents to American hegemony.[16]

The problem of reformism without reforms is reinforced by the crisis of political representation that the war in Iraq underlined. More than 20 million people in Europe demonstrated against the war, with the support of often large majorities in the opinion polls, only, in countries like Britain, Italy and Spain, to see their governments defy public opinion and support Bush, and elsewhere to have supposedly anti-war leaders such as Jacques Chirac and Gerhard Schröder seek to parley their position on Iraq into bargaining power in their diplomatic manoeuvres with Bush.

The anti-capitalist movement therefore needs, not simply to recognise the existence of, but to intervene in, the political field as a distinctive social reality with its specific constraints and forms of power.[17] The fact that Cassen and his supporters in France sought unsuccessfully to run an altermondialiste slate in the European parliamentary elections of June 2004 is a grudging acknowledgement of this need. Elsewhere in Europe—notably the PRC in Italy and Respect in England and Wales—contested these elections on the basis that the anti-capitalist and anti-war movements demanded political representation.[18]

Space or movement?

The developing political and ideological differentiation within the movement is associated with disagreements about how it should organise. Both Cassen and Chico Whitaker of the Brazil-based Secretariat of the World Social Forum have argued strongly that the WSF and other social forums must function as a 'space' rather than (in the phrase widely used since Seattle) 'a movement of movements'. Whitaker offers a rather poetic statement of the difference:

A movement congregates people—its militants, as the militants of a party—who decide to organise themselves to accomplish, collectively, certain objectives. Its formation and existence entail the definition of strategies to reach these objectives, the formulation of action programmes and the distribution of responsibilities among its members—including those concerning the direction of the movement... Its organisational structure is necessarily pyramidal, however democratic the internal process of decision and the way used to choose those who will occupy the different levels of management might be. On the other hand, its efficacy will depend on the explicitness and precision of its specific objectives and, therefore, of its own delimitation, in time and space.

A space has no leaders. It's only a place, basically horisontal, just like the earth's surface, despite admitting ups and downs. It's like a square without owner—if the square has an owner other than the collectivity, it fails to be a square, becoming a private territory. The squares are generally open spaces that can be visited by all those who find any kind of interest in using it. Their purpose is solely being a square, whichever is the service they render to its users. The more they last as squares the better for those who avail themselves of what these offer to the realisation of their respective objectives.

On the other hand, even when a square contains trees and small hills, it is always a socially horisontal space. The one who climbs the trees or the hills cannot intend, from high above, to control, neither entirely nor even partially, the actions of those inside the square. Being considered ridiculous by the others on the square is the least the climber should expect. Should he become insistent or inconvenient, he will end up by talking to himself, for the visitors will leave the square—or even come back with 'public authorities' who will make him leave or stop preaching from above, restoring the peace and tranquility typical of the public squares.[19]

Whitaker accordingly insists that the social forums must be seen as 'a space able to incubate movements'. Defending the same conception, Cassen expresses strong reservations about the militant tone of the process leading up to the first ESF in Florence and accuses activists from the LCR and the SWP of seeking to turn the social forums into 'a Fifth International'. He expresses particular suspicion of the Assembly of the Social Movements that has met regularly at each WSF and ESF. This body is indeed in part a device for evading the ban on social forums taking decisions that is inscribed in the WSF Charter of Principles. The Assembly of the Social Movements has no right to speak on behalf of the Social Forum and its participants. The calls that it issues merely bind the activists present and the organisations represented at the Assembly that choose to be so bound. Probably the most important of these calls were issued in 2002: in Porto Alegre in January, representing a powerful commitment of the movement to resisting war as well as neo-liberalism, and in Florence in November, where 15 February 2003 was declared an international day of anti-war protest. But Cassen criticises the Italian organisers of the ESF in Florence for taking the Porto Alegre call as their reference point and Florence itself for 'having taken a "movement" connotation rather than a "space" one', and for the prominence of the radical left.[20]

Cassen and Whitaker must between them take much of the credit for the original initiative that led to the first World Social Forum meeting in Porto Alegre in January 2001.[21] Their views are worth taking seriously, and some of the more detailed points that they make (for example, that the enormous effort putting in organising and selecting speakers for the large—and often tedious—plenary 'conferences' at the ESF and WSF is a waste of time and resources) are well taken. Though Cassen is scathing in dismissal of the 'No Vox' coalition that groups together many French autonomists, the contrast between 'space' and 'movement' has been taken up in autonomist circles, which now also often use Whitaker's opposition between 'horisontal' and 'vertical' to differentiate themselves from the radical left within the anti-capitalist movement.

But these contrasts aren't really tenable. To begin with, as Whitaker himself concedes, the social forums are 'not a neutral space'. The WSF Charter of Principles defines itself 'in opposition to a process of globalisation commanded by the large multinational corporations and by the governments and international institutions at the service of those corporations' interests'. So this 'open space' isn't open to everyone: corporate capitalists and their servants aren't welcome. More important, the effort sharply to counterpose space and movement seeks crudely to break up the subtle interplay between debate and mobilisation through which resistance to neo-liberalism and war has developed. The success of the first WSF at the beginning of 2001 would have been inconceivable without the Seattle protests. In Europe it was the dynamic that led from Genoa to Florence and then on to 15 February that made the ESF a powerful force. Artificially to separate discussion space and mass movement would be completely to misunderstand what has brought us to where we are.

The opposition between vertical and horisontal is similarly in need of deconstruction. Whitaker's portrayal of the open space of the forums as leaderless and horisontal is a bit like a classical realist novel that takes for granted but conceals the existence of an omniscient narrator. Whitaker, in other words, writes himself out of the story. Cassen in this respect is more honest: in describing the origins of the WSF, he gives a detailed account of the role played by him, Whitaker, and the other leaders of the eight organisations that initially launched the WSF and that continue to constitute its Secretariat. So the 'socially horisontal space' of the social forums has a notably 'vertical' moment (perhaps Whitaker thinks of the Secretariat as the 'public authorities' who are necessary to police the space, maybe to keep left wing agitators from getting out of hand). Cassen complains that the preparations for the ESF in Florence reflected a consensus of 'essentially three forces: the Italian and British "delegations" and the French representatives'.[22] But it's unclear why in principle this is more objectionable than the role played by the WSF Secretariat—except that Cassen politically prefers the decisions made by the latter. The origins of 15 February lay in an initiative taken by Italian and British activists—against bitter resistance from French delegates—at the ESF European Preparatory Assembly in Barcelona in October 2002.

Leadership of some kind is inherent in any large-scale social movement—and, whether Cassen and Whitaker like it or not, the social forums are part of the 'movement of movements'. The danger with the rhetoric of openness and horisontality is that it can make the real leadership secret and unaccountable. The gap between rhetoric and reality is illustrated when Cassen argues that the high-profile presence of a large number of French politicians at the second WSF in January 2002 had various positive consequences for the Forum.[23] Fair enough, but then why insist on the hypocritical ban on political parties in the WSF Charter of Principles, which has been circumvented from the start and which therefore can only feed cynicism? As we have seen, a movement on the scale of Seattle, Genoa and 15 February inevitably requires political articulation—or, rather, competing political articulations. The role arrogated for the Assembly of the Social Movements by some activists is in part a response to the way in which the dominant ideology of the social forums impedes political debate. It would seem much better to allow different political currents openly to articulate their visions and strategies.

Cassen points out correctly that many self-proclaimed 'social movements' have no real social base and highlights what he calls 'the 20 million person question':

Alex Callinicos

111

For this is really the central question, but not only for the forums: neither trade unions nor parties reach the real France 'from below': that of those about 20 million people— unemployed, poor blue and white collar workers, small shopkeepers eliminated by the supermarkets, single-parent families, people in insecure jobs, immigrants, etc—who are 'without' effective access to citisenship. Some of them despair

*of public action and, at election time (if they have the vote),
don't go to the polls or vote National Front. These people are
neither organised nor represented, but it is, however, above
all for them that the struggles for another globalisation are
fought. For them, but largely without them...*[24]

Cassen is absolutely right that the real challenge—and
not just in France—is to involve the victims of neo-liberal capitalism in a movement where they become
agents of their own emancipation. But the way in
which the anti-capitalist movement makes decisions is
itself an obstacle to involving the really oppressed and
exploited of our societies. In the process through
which social forums are organised (as opposed to the
forums themselves), where decisions have to be taken,
the consensus principle rules. Increasingly elaborate
theorisations have been developed about the 'method-
ology' of 'the process', according to which openness is
held to require taking decisions by consensus. It may
well be true that, in the early phases of the development of the anti-capitalist movement, making decisions by consensus helped to build trust among the
very diverse actors involved. But experience of the ESF
process confirms that consensus decision-making has
very great weaknesses. First of all, the effort to reach
consensus can make for very long, boring meetings.
Secondly, the need to arrive at decisions can encourage
manipulation and bargaining among the most powerful players that bypasses open discussion. Finally, at
worst, consensus decision-making can allow a destructive minority to hold process to ransom.

These defects mean that, although consensus
decision-making is justified by appeal to values such
as pluralism, transversality and inclusivity, it actually
works against participation. Lengthy meetings and

endless fights over decisions and the process itself drive many people away. The result is, at best, a kind of participatory bureaucracy that selects in favour of full time activists and that involves a social bias against the involvement of working class people, who lack the time to indulge in the protracted processes required and whose experience of their own trade union organisations habituates them to procedures that, though often formalistic and bureaucratic, do allow effective decisions to be taken by majority vote. A movement that seeks to change the world cannot afford to make a fetish of organisational norms that, whatever they may have contributed in the past, are becoming an increasingly serious barrier to its further development.

After Mumbai

Nevertheless, the key to addressing Cassen's '20 million person question' is political rather than organisational. It requires us to learn the right lessons from the short but dramatic history of the anti-capitalist movement. The trajectory of the movement from Genoa to the fourth World Social Forum in Mumbai in January 2004 has involved it simultaneously growing in size and becoming politically more radical. The Mumbai WSF was a particularly impressive event, taking place as it did in one of the great cities of Third World capitalism, in a country then ruled by a Hindu chauvinist party but also with powerful left organisations of a predominantly Stalinist (either orthodox Communist or Maoist) background that participated in the forum. It was a stunning success, far away the most socially representative of all the social forums, attracting 100,000 people, overwhelmingly from the poorest and oppressed sections of Indian society, while maintaining a militant tone: resisting the occupation of Iraq was the dominant theme of the vast opening ceremony, stressed especially by the writer and activist Arundhati Roy and Jeremy Corbyn of the Stop the War Coalition in Britain.[25]

The case of Mumbai underlines a paradox. Cassen and his supporters essentially pose a dilemma: the movement has to choose between becoming more radical and larger and more socially representative. But this is a false dilemma. The obvious example is the war in Iraq. This was a tougher, potentially more divisive issue than cancelling Third World debt or controlling international capital movements. But, at the same time, had the anti-capitalist movement failed to take it on, it would have been weakened, exposed as a marginal force with nothing to say about what remains the dominant issue in world politics. Not simply did the movement rise to this challenge while maintaining its unity, but it vastly increased its mobilising power with the great demonstrations on 15 February 2003.[26]

Of course, not everyone who turned out against the invasion of Iraq was also resisting the logic of neo-liberal capitalism: one of the most popular placards on the Hyde Park march had the characteristically English slogan 'Make Tea Not War'. But 15 February wasn't just a flash in the pan: the movement has shown a continuing capacity to mobilise against the occupation of Iraq. In his assessment of the Mumbai WSF Achin Vanaik argues that the call announced at the closing ceremony for a day of international protest on 20 March 2004, the first anniversary of the invasion of Iraq, 'will be a major test. It is unlikely that these [demonstrations] will reach the level of 15 February last year. Demanding an end to the US occupation worldwide will not mobilise all the constituencies that were prepared to come out before the war. But a million marching world-wide would be an undoubted step forward for anti-imperialist forces.'[27] In the event, this target was easily exceeded—two million people marched against the occupation in Rome alone, half a million in Madrid, 100,000 each in London and New York, confirming the vitality of the anti-capitalist and anti-war movements.

Experience thus suggests that it is by accepting the tough challenges presented by political events that the movement will continue to grow. In this sense, we can reject Cassen's dilemma: addressing the '20 million person question' does not require us to reject radical options. This doesn't mean we should instead pursue militancy for its own sake. The remarkable degree of unity that has been forged is a precious achievement that needs to be preserved. For example, the second ESF in Paris in November 2003 was notable for the involvement of mainstream trade unions that played at best a marginal role in Florence; the London ESF is likely to take this further.

The trajectory of the movement has involved growing in size and becoming politically more radical

Alex Callinicos

115

Moreover, behind the ridiculous ban on parties, a remarkable convergence has taken place between political actors from diverse, and indeed divergent, backgrounds. One striking ingredient in the success of the Mumbai WSF was the willingness of the Indian left parties, often with lamentable traditions of theoretical dogmatism and mutual sectarianism, to work constructively, not merely with each other, but with European Trotskyists. Parallel processes have taken place in the European radical left, as organisations with very different histories such as the PRC, the SWP and the LCR have come together within the anti-capitalist movement. None of this has been easy, and there have been

setbacks, but the renegotiation of once antagonist political identities is, let us hope, irreversible.

The real challenge for the movement, then, is how
to continue this dynamic, in which this movement has
simultaneously maintained its unity, faced up to the
tough political challenges with which it has been confronted, and grown in size and social reach. There is no
simple formula that will allow us successfully to
address this challenge. Walden Bello and Focus on the
Global South are undoubtedly right to stress the con-
nections between the issues that first gave birth to the
movement—in particular, the liberalisation of trade
and investment—and the imperialist occupation of
Iraq. Thus Bello argues that 'the Iraqi resistance has
transformed the global equation' by overextending US
imperialism and therefore making it harder for Washington to drive through further bouts of liberalisation.
This underlines the importance of building a movement that fights both neo-liberal economics and imperialist war.

The interplay between politics and economics
goes, however, much deeper than this. Our capacity to
defeat neo-liberalism depends critically on the extent
to which we are able to mobilise those who[28] are not
simply victims of the prevailing economic orthodoxy
but have the collective strength to defeat it—the
organised working class. It is surely not an accident
that the European country where the anti-capitalist
movement is strongest is Italy, which has seen both
giant anti-war protests and mass strikes against the
Berlusconi government's economic policies. This contrasts with, on the hand, Britain, where the anti-war
movement is strong but the economic class struggle
has still to recover from the terrible defeats suffered by
the workers' movement under Thatcher, and, on the

other, France, which experienced in May-June 2003 major mass strikes against the Chirac-Raffarin government's pension 'reform', but where opposition to the 'war on terrorism' has been comparatively weak. Much depends on whether economic and political struggles develop and fuse in a common movement against the capitalist system itself. In the words of Rosa Luxemburg, 'where the chains of capitalism are forged, there they must be broken.'[29]

Notes

1   For earlier assessments of the movement, see C Harman, 'Anti-Capitalism: Theory and Practice', **International Socialism**, 2.88 (2000); A Callinicos, 'Where Now?', in E Bircham and J Charlton (eds), **Anti-Capitalism: A Guide to the Movement** (London, 2001); A Callinicos, 'The Anti-Capitalist Movement after Genoa and New York', in S Aronowitz and H Gautney (eds), **Implicating Empire** (New York, 2003); and A Callinicos, **An Anti-Capitalist Manifesto** (Cambridge, 2003). T Mertes (ed), **A Movement of Movements** (London, 2004) is a valuable connection of interviews with leading intellectuals and activists.

2   A Negri and A Dufourmantelle, **Negri on Negri** (New York, 2004), p76.

3   Dominique Reynié, **La Fracture Occidentale** (Paris, 2004). These figures are, if anything, an underestimate, since Reynié says that 800,000 took part in the giant London march to Hyde Park on 15 February 2003, a conservative figure contradicted by survey evidence that 1.25 million British households had at least one member on the march.

4   An important exception here is provided by the writings of Walden Bello, who has consistently shown a concern for the strategic direction of the movement.

5   Available at www.forumsocialmundial.org.br.

6   See A Callinicos, **Anti-Capitalist Manifesto**, ch 2.

7   A Callinicos, 'The Anti-Capitalist Movement after Genoa and New York', as above, p139.

8   P Khalfa, 'La Guerre en Iraq, et Après?', **Le Grain de Sable**, no 422, 9 May 2003, www.attac.org

9   M Hardt, 'Folly of Our Masters of the Universe', **Guardian**, 18 December 2002.

10 B Cassen, 'On the Attack', **New Left Review** (II) 19 (2003), p53.

11 M Hardt, 'A Trap Set for Protestors', **Guardian**, 21 February 2003.

12 See A Callinicos, **The New Mandarins of American Power** (Cambridge, 2003), and D Harvey, **The New Imperialism** (Oxford, 2003).

13 See G Monbiot, **The Age of Consent** (London, 2003), and, for a more cautious version of the same kind of strategy, D Held and A McGrew, **Globalization/Anti-Globalization** (Cambridge, 2002).

14 Khalfa, 'La Guerre en Iraq, et Après?'

15 B Cassen, 'Trois Questions pour ATTAC', May 2003, www.france.attac.org

16 M Hardt and A Negri, 'Why We Need a Multilateral Magna Carta', **Global Agenda**, 2004, www.globalagendamagazine.com. Compare Z Brzezinski, **The Choice** (New York, 2004).

17 Stathis Kouvelakis argues that the revolutionary left in France has suffered since the mid-1990s from a tendency towards an 'anti-political' approach: 'A New Political Cycle', **International Socialist Tendency Discussion Bulletin** no 5, July 2004, www.istendency.net

18 A Callinicos, 'The European Radical Left Tested Electorally', in J Rees and A Callinicos **Building the Party in the Age of Mass Movements** (SWP 2004).

19 C Whitaker, 'Notes about the World Social Forum', 17
    March 2003, available at www.forumsocialmundial.org.br

20 Cassen, **Tout a Commencé à Porto Alegre...** (Paris,
    2003), ch 3 (quotation from p124), a bizarrely detailed
    discussion of meetings that is very hard to follow
    unless you were one of the handful of activists who
    attended most of them.

21 Cassen gives an interesting account of the foundation
    of the WSF in B Cassen, as above, chs 1 and 2.

22 As above, p125.

23 As above, pp83-88.

24 As above, pp139-140.

25 See A Callinicos, 'A Festival of the Oppressed', 23 January
    2004, newstandard.newsnet, and A Vanaik, 'Rendezvous
    at Mumbai', **New Left Review** (II) 26 (2004).

26 This isn't the only tough political issue the movement
    has had to confront. After the violent confrontations
    between protesters and police at the Gothenburg and
    Genoa summits in the summer of 2001, leading figures
    in ATTAC France argued that there should be no more
    demonstrations. The wave of mass protests against the
    repression in Genoa that swept through Italy in the
    summer of 2001 and then merged into the first anti-
    war marches was a tacit answer to this proposal. One
    of the achievements of the Florence ESF was that on 9
    November 2002 a million people marched against the
    coming war in Iraq without the violence and destruction
    that the Berlusconi government and its mouthpieces
    claimed would engulf the city.

27 A Vanaik, 'Rendezvous at Mumbai', as above, p65.

28 W Bello, 'Empire and Resistance Today', 25 June 2004,
    www.zmag.org

29 R Luxemburg, 'Our Programme and the Political
    Situation', in **Selected Political Writings** (ed D Howard,
    New York, 1971), p397.

Prabir Purkayastha is a founding member of the Delhi Science Forum. He was on the organising committee for the World Social Forum held in Mumbai 2004 and the Asian Social Forum. www.delhiscienceforum.org

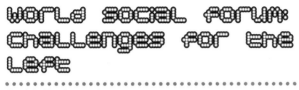

World Social Forum: Challenges for the Left

Prabir Purkayastha

From Porto Alegre in 2001 to Mumbai this year
the World Social Forum has been not just a march of
ideas through different countries and continents but
also a joining together of different strands of the anti-
imperialist platform. If Florence and the European
Social Forum in 2002 fused the anti-war movement to
the struggle against neo-liberalism, Mumbai and the
WSF2004 brought in other issues such as race, patri-
archy and caste. All of this has brought together a large
number of groups and movements, who, even though
they oppose the current neo-liberal and militarist
agenda perhaps would not have easily shared a common space.

In organisational terms also, the spread of the
WSF to different parts of the world has allowed different forms of organisation and therefore an exchange
of experiences between activists of a kind which otherwise would not have taken place. However, such a

major expression of global solidarity cannot be organised without discussing serious questions regarding its future. What is the nature of the WSF: is it to be a transitional platform to a more well defined organisation for global action? Or is it an open space for reflective thinking, something to be kept in its current format in perpetuity? Or is there a third way that allows the reflective open space character of the WSF to continue and yet allow organised global actions to emerge? To my mind, this is the critical issue that we need as activists to address. Only then will the other issues around the WSF—its character, its focus and the nature of organisation—be open to a critical examination.

The WSF was conceived as a response to the growing struggle against neo-liberal globalisation. While a number of events may be cited as the precursor, the Seattle protests against the WTO were perhaps the defining moment in the birth of the WSF. The response of Seattle protests and the growing global disillusionment with neo-liberal reforms was the backdrop of the first Social Forum. The second important milestone was the protests in Genoa in July 2001, where the Genoa Social Forum played a critical role. Various groups around the world increasingly felt that without global coordination and action it could not push back the offensive of global capital. Local actions, while extremely important, were not enough. These groups were heterogeneous: they came from diverse political and social streams, had different historical experiences. The open space character of the WSF allowed for this heterogeneity to be retained: groups could meet without losing their identity.

Open space and heterogeneity of movements today

There is little doubt that without an open space concept the WSF would not have had its current reach. The ability of people to come to the WSF, be critical of others, and not be party to a common declaration allowed a whole range of groups from different parts of the world to come to Porto Alegre. All of us, who have been involved with the WSF in its various stages, were surprised by the extent of enthusiasm for such a forum. If the Brazilian organising committee were taken aback by the participation of much larger numbers than they had anticipated both in 2001 and 2002, we in India were equally surprised by the numbers, both for the Asian Social Forum in Hyderabad and subsequently for the WSF2004 in Mumbai. The response to the ESF in Florence also far exceeded the expectations of the organisers there. I am sure London will be no different in this respect. Therefore, those who see in the open space concept only amorphousness and a dilution of the ideology perhaps need to view the concept differently.

The WSF space should not be misconstrued as a completely open space: it is an oppositional space to imperialist globalisation. The space that the WSF provides is, however, a contended one. The large number of different views, experiences and ideological positions vie with each other. To some, opposition to globalisation is limited to generating critiques of institutions of imperialist globalisation—to others the WSF must open up to action and the overthrow of these institutions. To some, it is a conscious space to promote civil society and social movements. To others, it is a step towards building a global network and movements. The entire spectrum of the groups within this oppositional space does not constitute then a

Prabir
Purkayastha

homogenous and harmonious whole. It is also linked to the reality that, while the slogan of 'Another world is possible' is attractive as a rejection of today's neo-liberal order, any world that comes into being out of the multiplicity of alternates can only be a singular one. This future may contain a plurality of views but not a plurality of worlds.

To those who would restrict the WSF to only a reflective space in which critiques are placed, the transformation of the world to a new one is outside the scope of the WSF. The social democrats and most NGOs believe that the WSF should be a primarily a reflective space and there should be no action agenda there. While they argue that it should be open space, they also are quite uncomfortable with organised left movements entering the WSF in any form. In their view, the WSF should provide some kind of 'feel good' space, and be limited to civil society organisations. Their conscious attempt in all this is to project small groups and movements as the real people's movements, as distinct from the organised left and class based organisations.

To those of us who are in the struggle for such a socialist transformation, we should not restrict this open space from the other side, but make it a movement or action-friendly space. It should actively facilitate a programmes agenda without itself becoming such a platform. The need is therefore for consciously privileging movements and the experience of different kinds of resistance within the reflective space. It is this conscious shift that the WSF is not just another academic space but to a space for reflection on how to change the world. And this links up to what we have discussed earlier that finally there is only one future world, even if there are alternate worlds on view in the WSF based on the different worldview of the groups.

If we take it as given that the WSF should not be limited to only a reflective space but also should facilitate global anti-imperialist struggles, should it itself become an organisation for conducting such struggles? In my view, the WSF itself should not be seen to be an organisation which either builds or leads such struggles. This distinction is important, as those who are constructing this open space for movements should not end up by substituting themselves for the movements. The distinction between the WSF organisers organising the space while the movements organise the activities/ action plan should continue. The WSF organisers are not necessarily of the movements: the WSF organisers should not compete with movements for space. Any success in building a global anti-imperialist struggle depends on the movements coming together, both politically and in organisational terms. And by virtue of building a WSF event, the organisers should not get privileged over the movements.

Networked structure and polycentric events

The movements in various countries are the spearhead of struggle against imperialism—either its militaristic, coercive version or its more insidious economic version. The WSF, as a platform, enables these movements to come together—as either one network or a multiple set of networks—in order to take this struggle forward. For this, the WSF space can be consciously constructed to bring together the concerns, experiences, information and issues of diverse movements and groups, and also catalyse the formation of networks around these issues.

The WSF has provided this kind of an environment

and this has helped in revitalising and radicalising the anti-imperialist struggle internationally. Some of it is already visible in synchronising the anti Iraq War struggle in different countries—demonstrations, protests on the same day throughout the world—and in working out a common understanding regarding the Cancun Ministerial. The European Social Forum in Florence fused the anti-war and the anti-imperialist globalisation concerns and has helped radicalise the WSF. It has put social democracy in Europe at a disadvantage as some sections of social democracy have supported NATO and the US war agenda. Even today social democracy's stand on nuclear weapons and imperialist interventions is ambiguous. The anti-war agenda thus has created a larger space for left and radical forces internationally.

What various groups and individuals have to address is the emergence of loose networks, which are able to bring together activists not only in terms of ideas but also in terms of action. Hitherto people have taken for granted that action requires centralised organisational structures. However, the WSF structure brings out an important emerging element: the importance of flat, networked structures in synchronising action as well as in politically integrating ideas.

But can we look at networked structures, not as a substitute but as a complement for other structures that exist? Of course such structures have their limitations and so does representative democracy within such structures. They can be taken over by large well-heeled organisations. But as long as other structures exist and there are multiple centres, such networked structures can continue to play a vital role in the dynamic of the anti-imperialist movements today. It is perhaps necessary for us to see how we can work creatively within such structures.

The social movement assemblies in the WSF have undoubtedly provided a focus for an action agenda. The social movement's assembly in the Florence ESF, certainly was crucial in synchronisation of the anti-war demonstrations worldwide. Some of the groups believe that an over-arching activists assembly or a social movements assembly helps in building the movement space while not impinging on the WSF's open, reflective space character. Others have considered the social movements assembly another attempt by some political groups to build a new international. The bogey of the traditional left usurping the open space has already been raised in this context. With the experience of the ASF and the WSF2004, I believe that an all-encompassing social movements/activists assembly as the only movement space may be too limiting on one hand in terms of space and too ambitious on the other in terms of organising a single movement space for all activists. There are two possible ways of getting around this, both of which are not mutually exclusive:

Prabir
Purkayastha

a: We look not only to one social movement space but to creating multiple such spaces: anti-war, anti-WTO, trade unions, women, etc.
b: We try to incorporate the activists' agenda in the programme itself.

I am sure that both these strategies will be used in the WSF to enhance its movement-friendly character. Otherwise, the WSF will lose its centrality in the growing international solidarity of movements against imperialist globalisation.

One of the changes made in the WSF2004 in Mumbai from the earlier format was to create a larger space for self-organised events. They were not only invited for seminars and workshops but also for organising panels and conferences. This helped in creating not just one centre of power for the event but multiple ones, with groups coming together for their events. The selection of the self-organised events was based not on the thematic content alone but to help promote diversity.

To generalise, WSF events should be seen as polycentric events. Various groups can get together and organise around certain issues. These should not be just seen as themes but could be on the trajectory, for example of the anti-war movements. Space could be provided not only for well known critics of imperialist war such as Noam Chomsky but also ask the major anti-war coalitions in various countries to present their experience. Such an approach can avoid both the criticisms: how not to be just a talking shop and also not to be seen as building a new international.

The WSF and its evolution

It needs to be underlined that the WSF emerged, not out of a single planned process, but out of a large number of processes. In fact, when the first WSF was organised in 2001, it had not been planned that it would become a regular event. As the WSF has grown in size and influence, it has naturally thrown up a number of questions regarding its future direction.

The evolution of the WSF now must face questions on how do mega-events, drawing huge numbers from different parts of the world help in building this new world, even if the architecture of this world is not defined and its contours contested? Does the forum need to take place every year? Is it possible to keep on holding forums with a constantly growing number of participants? What are the alternatives available in view of what is being called the forum's 'gigantism'?

Today the World Social Forum process needs to take stock of where this huge exercise is leading. Many participants at the forum in 2003 and 2004 felt that the forum is becoming too large and unmanageable, putting inordinate pressure on resources, and losing a sense of focus. The forum has already responded to the need to further broaden the process and ensure larger participation of people from different parts. The first three forums in Porto Alegre had seen participation of larger and larger numbers (15,000 in 2001, 50,000 in 2002 and 100,000 in 2003) but the participation from Asia and Africa had remained small—a couple of thousand from two continents that represent two thirds of humanity. This was the background of the decision to have the WSF2004 in India.

The exercise of decentralising the WSF process that was initiated in 2002 must continue. This led to the organisation of regional and thematic forums. Some of these too were huge successes, like the European Social Forum in Florence and the Asian Social Forum in Hyderabad. Today a large number of regional forums—European, Asian, African, Mediterranean, Caribbean, American and many country forums are being organised regularly. Much of the vitality of the WSF is derived from this and not necessarily from the central event. In the International Council meeting of the WSF in 2003 January, many members articulated the need to consider whether the WSF should continue to be held as an annual event. Many also felt that the huge size of the global event, while lending strength to the opposition to imperialist globalisation, also tends to inhibit fruitful interactions that can contribute to the development of concrete alternatives.

Sooner rather than later the WSF will have to convert its annual event to once in two years if not three. The scope for more of the same event but bigger has its obvious limitations. However, this conversion to a less frequent event must be accompanied by either regional/country or more focused thematic forums. This will allow more and more groups to be drawn into a set of common networks and will also allow action plans to emerge either around issues or at the local level.

Finally, the left must realise that its constituency today is far larger than its organised reach. Whether it is the WSF or the anti-war marches, people are willing to join in the struggle against anti-imperialist globalisation and war. We can continue to be prisoners of our past and think in terms of our narrow organisational reach or have the confidence to reach out to the people. And along with changing the world, we might also have to change ourselves as well. This is the challenge that all of us face, whether in the European Social Forum or in other similar platforms.

Luciana Genro is a founding member of P-SOL (the socialism and freedom party), and a federal deputy in the Brazilian parliament. She was expelled from the PT (Workers Party) for voting against Lula's government plans to attack public sector workers' pensions.
www.psol.org.br

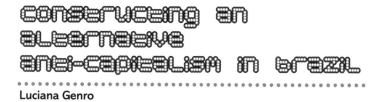

Constructing an alternative anti-capitalism in Brazil

Luciana Genro

The fight against capitalism in Latin America has been expressed in several ways. Bolivia, Ecuador and Argentina, for example, have seen insurrections that brought down governments which damaged their people with neo-liberal policies. Unemployment, low wages, privatisation, the sell-out of the country, were reasons that brought thousands of people onto the streets in great democratic and anti-imperialist struggles.

These battles and insurrections were not able to forge a leadership in the working class which was capable of guiding people to take power into their own hands. Through elections, governments promising change took office and capitulated to the interests of imperialism. However, the people go on fighting and the challenge of building anti-capitalist parties with influence among the masses is the order of the day.

Undoubtedly the process is most developed in

Venezuela and it is the one we should draw to the attention of both Latin American fighters and the rest of the world. Since the 'Caracazo' took place, a popular manifestation that threw out Carlos Andrés' government, there has started a process which has been through many different stages and has been generally called the Bolivarian revolution. This process is still in development and it has not defined its class character precisely. The idea of the Bolivarian revolution expresses a sense of transformation and a process of development. But anyway Chávez and Chavismo today, even with its mediation, contradictions and limitations, is a fundamental part in the fight against the plans of North American imperialism for recolonisation. The idea of the integration of Latin America that has now been defended by thousands and thousands of Bolivarian militants and many workers' and popular organisations is enormously progressive in standing up to imperialism in the continent and in contributing to the process of building an anti-capitalist alternative. We can say that Bolivarianism has rekindled the idea that we are part of a continental confrontation that has passed through different periods and stages.

We are facing an imperialist plan of recolonisation and it will not stop because it responds to the critical course of the process of capitalist accumulation. This obliges the United States to guarantee its hegemony, raising the level of exploitation and robbery, especially in Latin America which the US regards as its 'backyard'. This is the context of the confrontation, although limited still, between Chávez and North American imperialism. This confrontation in Venezuela itself is expressed in a battle between social classes. On one side are the big bourgeoisie and sections of the middle classes who go along with it and on the other side are those who name themselves 'new social subjects' and have entered the fight in Latin America. This way, the old tradition of struggle in our continent, and in particular working class struggle, has brought in the great number of socially excluded that capitalist misery produces: the poor people in the cities, the peasants and the unemployed.

In Venezuela these are concentrated especially in the huge population which lives in slums that surround the centre of Caracas. We are faced with an open process that will depend on the development of mass mobilisation in this particular country, but also on how the resistance to imperialism in Latin America generalises, and on the new uprisings that will certainly occur in our continent in the next few years.

People elected Lula, believing he would provide the changes everybody wanted. The opposite occurred

Luciana Genro

135

Brazil is going through a different situation. The feeling against capitalism and against neo-liberalism was not expressed in an uprising of the masses. It was channelled by the PT by institutional means. People elected Lula, believing he would provide the changes everybody was hoping for. The opposite occurred. The PT allied with oligarchies, with the international market and with North American imperialism so that the neo-liberal capitalist model could continue, now bolstered by the credibility of the working class leader who for decades denounced unemployment and wage freezes.

The PT, which has been the biggest left party in Latin America and a reference point for the left around the world, became an instrument to apply policies against the working class.

We were only four parliamentarians who dared to

denounce this and who refused to put our mandates, which the working class gave us, at the service of the interests of big capital: myself, Baba, João Fontes and Senator Heloísa Helena, who because of her political views, her charisma and her strength has become one of the most popular leaders in the country. But if inside the parliament we were few, on the streets we are many. We are an impressive vanguard, which wants to make sure that deception doesn't turn to paralysis or prostration.

First was the strike of the public sector workers against pension reform, with their demonstrations that put around 80,000 people on the streets of Brasilia. Challenging its historical leaders and the majority of the CUT leadership, which is totally co-opted by the government and transformed into its auxiliary inside the trade union movement, the government workers went out to the streets and showed an extraordinary willingness to fight.

This break of some of the masses with the government began just months after Lula took over the presidency. From this moment on it kept going deeper as the attacks on the working class kept happening, with the imposition of a starvation minimum wage, trade union reform and university reform, and also with the continuation of the old practices of corruption and embezzlement. The most recent case was the president of the central bank, accused of sending money abroad illegally and hiding funds. He received ministerial immunity from Lula to hinder the investigations. We should remember that this gentleman, installed in the economic heart of the country, has spent his whole professional life in service for the Bank of Boston, the main institution responsible for the Brazil's external debt and the provider of a generous pension to him.

It is in this context that P-SOL, the Socialism and Freedom Party, was created. Faced with the incontrovertible need to continue the fight against capitalism, the deputies expelled from the PT joined trade unionists, militants from the social movements and important intellectuals in Brazilian universities, and in June of this year we founded P-SOL.

This new party is a component of a new experience, going beyond the PT to unite all those who were not seduced by the siren calls of neo-liberalism and who strongly believe in the necessity and possibility of carrying on the fight against capitalism.

We believe in defending the concrete demands of the working class: wages, employment, agrarian reform, defence of public services and of the basic rights of the workers. In order to accomplish that, we insist on the need to break with the IMF, refuse to pay the external debt, control exchange rates and restrict the movement of capital. We also think it is necessary to take over the big conglomerates and capitalist monopolies and renationalise the companies privatised during the 1990s.

Our provisional programme, voted on in our meeting in June, is not a complete revolutionary one. However, it includes essential themes for the construction of an anti-capitalist party with influence in the masses that has the capacity to unite the Brazilian socialist left. At the same time, it intends to give support to the construction of an international expression of the forces opposed to capitalism.

The basis of our programme clearly locates the defence of socialism with democracy as a strategic principle for overcoming the capitalist order, rejecting the authoritarian variants of so called 'real socialism'. Located in a continent where the fight for national sovereignty is a matter of survival in the here and now, we participate in this struggle with a perspective of breaking capitalist domination. There is no real national independence without breaking with the basis of the capitalist economic model, with imperialism and with its forms of domination.

Our programme rejects class conciliation and governments in coalition with the bourgeoisie. This is another principle of our political building. The PT began its process of political degeneration governing together with the bourgeoisie and defending the idea of a 'government for all', many years before it came to power in the country.

Finally, our strategy demands that we take on the struggle for winning back the idea of internationalism, through our involvement in the movement against globalisation, with its social forums and its mobilisations started in Seattle. We denounce and oppose imperialist war, the occupations and invasions by the great capitalist powers, as in Iraq, and place ourselves unequivocally in the struggle for self-determination.

We know that the Brazilian process has repercussions in the international socialist left. The PT was rightly seen in its time by the international left as something different from the old European social democracy—as an independent party able to give voice to social movements in the battle with the bourgeois parties. The irreversible crisis of this project also obliges those who fight against capitalism all over the world to make new choices.

Those political sectors that still believe in the possibilities of change inside the PT are on the wrong side. It is impossible to construct an alternative against capitalism or build a socialist left inside a political party which is clearly playing the game of North American imperialism. Even worse is to accept being part of this government, as is the case with a sector of Democracia Socialista, which for many years was the strongest tendency defending socialist ideas inside the PT and is part of the Fourth International—the Unified Secretariat.

As if the economic policy in the service of the bankers and counter-reforms at the behest of the IMF are not enough, the clearest capitulation to Bush's interests is that Brazil has sent troops to Haiti. This was supported by the PT and was defended by the so called left PT deputies.

Because of this, we have no doubts: it is the duty of Brazilian socialists to provide a left opposition to the government of Lula, something that can only be done from outside the PT. We know that to build an anti-capitalist party with influence in the masses is no easy task. At the same time, we see day by day a huge space for the socialist left. We have confidence in the capacity for mobilisation among the working class in the renovation of its leading role, in the appearance of a new leadership which will replace the old leaders who have sold out and are too bureaucratic to organise the fight.

In going through this process we are also contributing to the reconstruction of the international left and of socialist thought. The neo-liberal surge of the decade of the 90s and the apparent 'final victory' of capitalism weakened the ideas of socialism. It was one of the reasons that opportunism showed itself so confidently and why (along with material inducements) a large part of the Brazilian left converted to the politics of social liberalism. But the paradox is that the same globalisation process has aggravated all the most basic

P-SOL is going beyond the PT to unite all those not seduced by the siren calls of neo-liberalism

Luciana Genro

139

contradictions of capitalism and undermined the foundations on which reformism and opportunism, which deny the possibility of socialist transformation, are built.

Globalisation has exposed all the explosive contradictions of the imperialist stage of capitalism which were hidden, especially in the big capitalist metropolis: the increase of poverty, chronic unemployment, the destruction of regions and countries, the new military stage of imperialism which has led to the new war of conquest against Iraq. In this situation, the conditions for the advance of socialist ideas across the whole world, that were absent for a long time, are now back.

Globalisation also created a powerful tool of resistance and struggle. The movement initiated in Seattle, and continued in the big mobilisations against globalisation since then, has joined with the powerful movement against the imperialist war in Iraq. The social forums represented a meeting point for discussion and coordination of the social movements that permitted the big mobilisations against the Iraq war.

We are in a moment where there are better conditions for the fight for socialism. We have reached a time when it is possible to advance in the regrouping of revolutionaries to build a point of reference which is anti-imperialist, internationalist and socialist. The forum in London will be a new meeting point for this. And pretty soon we will have another opportunity in the World Social Forum, in January of 2005, which will take a place in Porto Alegre, Brazil.

It will be a new opportunity for us to discuss and to make stronger links among the organisations of the international left and to pass on the experience from P-SOL. We know that our future will be played out in the international context. The experience from 'real socialism' also shows that imperialism can be definitely defeated only in the international arena. As Francisco de Oliveira, the important Brazilian sociologist and founder of the PT who today is putting his energies into founding P-SOL, asks, "Will the 21st century be socialist or not?"

Luciana Genro

Michael Albert is a co-founder of **Z Magazine** for which he is currently an editorial writer and columnist. His main activist focus has long been the creation and nurturing of alternative media institutions, particularly the internet. He is the author of many books including those with an emphasis on economic alternatives to capitalism. Recent writings include **Thinking Forward: Ten Lectures on Economic Vision**, **Thought Dreams: Radical Theory for the 21st Century** (2004) and **Parecon** (2003). Many of his writings are available on the web. www.zmag.org / www.parecon.org

beyond capitalism

Michael Albert

To build and take an anti-capitalist movement forward, as per the title of this book, we need to reject capitalism but also to advocate a new system in its place as well as to act in light of not only our critique of capitalism but also the strategic and organisational implications of our goals. What is a viable anti-capitalist vision? What immediate strategic implications can we draw from it?

Participatory economics instead of capitalism

Capitalism incorporates private ownership of the means of production, market allocation, and corporate divisions of labour. Capitalist remuneration is for property, power, and to a limited extent contribution to output. Class divisions under capitalism arise due to property and also due to differential access to empowered versus obedient work. Huge differences in decision-making influence and quality of circumstances flourish. Buyers and sellers one-up each other. The public reaps the social and ecological catastrophes that self-interested capitalist market competition sows.

To transcend capitalism, suppose we advocate common leftist core values: solidarity, diversity, equity, self-management and ecological sustainability. What institutions can propel these values as well as admirably accomplish economic functions?

To start, we might advocate public/social property relations in place of privatised capitalist property relations. In the new system, all citizens own each workplace in equal part. This ownership conveys no special right or income. Bill Gates doesn't own a massive proportion of the means by which software is produced. We all own it—or, symmetrically, no one owns it. At any rate, ownership becomes moot regarding distribution of income, wealth or power. In this way the ills of personal accrual of profits yielding huge wealth differentials disappear.

Next workers and consumers could be organised into democratic councils with the norm for decisions being that our methods of dispersing information to decision makers and of arriving at preferences and then tallying them into decisions should convey to each actor about each decision influence over the decision in proportion to the degree he or she will be affected by it.

Workers' and consumers' councils would be the seat of decision-making power and would exist at many levels, including sub-units such as work groups and teams and individuals, and supra-units such as workplaces and whole industries.

People in councils would be the economy's decision makers. Votes could be majority rule, three quarters, two thirds, consensus, etc. Votes would be taken at different levels, with fewer or more participants, depending on the particular implications of the decisions in question. Sometimes a team or individual would make a decision pretty much on its own. Sometimes a whole workplace or even a whole industry would be the decision body.

Different voting and tallying methods would be employed as needed for different decisions. There is no a priori single correct choice. There is, however, a right norm to try to efficiently and sensibly implement: decision-making input should be in proportion as one is affected by decisions.

> **We shouldn't get more by virtue of having more power or owning more property**

Next we alter the organisation of work by changing who does what tasks in what combinations. Each actor does a job, of course. Each job is composed of a variety of tasks, of course. What changes from current corporate divisions of labour to a preferred future division of labour is that the particular variety of tasks each actor does is balanced for its empowerment and quality of life implications.

Every person participating in creating new products is a worker. The combination of tasks and responsibilities you have at work accords you the same empowerment and quality of life as the combination I have accords me, and likewise for each other worker and their balanced job complex.

We do not have some people overwhelmingly monopolising empowering, fulfilling and engaging tasks and circumstances. We do not have other people overwhelmingly saddled with only rote, obedient and dangerous things to do. For reasons of equity and especially in order to create the conditions of democratic participation and self-management, when we each participate in our workplace and consumer decision making, we each have been comparably prepared by our work with confidence, skills, and knowledge to do so.

In contrast, the typical capitalist situation is that some people who produce (I want to call them the coordinator class) have great confidence, social skills, decision-making skills, and relevant knowledge imbued by their daily work situations, while other people who produce (who I want to call the working class) are only tired, deskilled, and without relevant decision-making knowledge due to their daily work situations.

Balanced job complexes do away with this division of circumstances and the associated class hierarchy. They complete the task of removing the root basis for class divisions that is begun by eliminating private ownership of capital. That is, they eliminate not only the role of owner/capitalist and the associated disproportionate power and wealth, but also the role of intellectual/decision maker with its excessive power and wealth. Balanced job complexes apportion conceptual and empowering and also rote and unempowering responsibilities in tune with true classlessness.

Next comes remuneration. We work. This entitles us to a share of the product of work. But the new participatory economic vision says that we ought to receive for our labours an amount in tune with how hard we have worked, how long we have worked, and with the sacrifices we have endured at work.

We shouldn't get more by virtue of being more productive due to having better tools, more skills or greater inborn talent, much less get more by virtue of having more power or owning more property.

We should be entitled to more consumption only by virtue of expending more of our effort or otherwise enduring more sacrifice. This is morally appropriate and it also provides proper incentives due to rewarding only what we can affect, not what we can't.

With balanced job complexes, for eight hours of normally paced work Sally and Sam receive the same income. This is the case whether they have the same job or any job at all. No matter what their particular job may be, no matter what workplaces they are in and how different their mix of tasks is, and no matter how talented they are. If they work at a balanced job complex, their total workload will be similar in its quality of life implications and empowerment effects, so the only difference relevant to reward for their labours is going to be length and intensity of work done, and with these also equal the share of output earned will be equal. If length of time working or intensity of working differ somewhat, so will share of output earned differ somewhat.

Who mediates decisions about job complexes and the rates people work at? Workers do, of course

Michael Albert

147

Who mediates decisions about the definition of job complexes and about what rates and intensities people are working? Workers do, of course, in their councils and with appropriate decision-making say using information culled by methods consistent with employing balanced job complexes and providing just remuneration.

There is one very large step remaining, even to offering only a broad outline of participatory economic vision. How are the actions of workers and consumers connected? How do decisions made in workplaces and by consumer councils, as well as by individual consumers, all come into accord?

What causes the total produced by workplaces to match the total consumed collectively by neighbourhoods and other groups and privately by individuals?

For that matter, what determines the relative social valuation of different products and choices? What decides how many workers will be in which industry producing how much? What determines whether some product should be made or not, and how much? What determines what investments in new productive means and methods should be undertaken and which other investments should be delayed or rejected? These are all matters of allocation.

Existing options for dealing with allocation are central planning (as was used in the old Soviet Union) and markets (as is used in all capitalist economies with minor or greater variations).

In central planning a bureaucracy culls information, formulates instructions, sends these instructions to workers and consumers, gets some feedback, refines the instructions a bit, sends them again, and gets back obedience.

In a market each actor in isolation from concern for other actors' wellbeing competitively pursues his or her own agenda by buying and selling labour (or the ability to do work) and buying and selling products and resources at prices determined by competitive bidding. Each person seeks to gain more than other parties in their exchanges.

The problem is that each of these two modes of connecting actors to accomplish allocation tasks imposes on the economy pressures that subvert the values we favour. Markets, even without private capitalisation of property, distort valuations to favour private over public benefits and to channel personalities in anti-social directions thereby diminishing and even destroying solidarity. They reward primarily output and power and not effort and sacrifice. They divide economic actors into a working class that is saddled with rote and obedient labour and another class, who I call the coordinator class, that enjoys empowering circumstances and determines economic outcomes while accruing most income. They isolate buyers and sellers as decision makers left with no option but to competitively ignore the wider implications of their choices, including effects on the ecology.

Central planning, in contrast, is authoritarian. It denies self-management and produces the same coordinator class / working class division and hierarchy as markets. With central planning the division is built first around the distinction between planners and those who implement their plans, and then extends outward to incorporate empowered and dis-empowered workers more generally.

The bottom line is that both these allocation systems subvert rather than propel classlessness. What is parecon's alternative to markets and central planning?

Suppose in place of top-down imposition of centrally planned choices and in place of competitive market exchange by atomised buyers and sellers, we opt for cooperative, informed choosing by organisationally and socially entwined actors each having a say in proportion as choices impact them, each able to access needed accurate information and valuations, and each having appropriate training and confidence to develop and communicate their preferences.

That combination of features could work compatibly with council-centered participatory self-management, remuneration for effort and sacrifice, balanced job complexes, proper valuations of collective and ecological impacts, and classlessness. To these ends, activists might therefore favour participatory

> **Economic vision is not enough, we also need political, cultural and gender-related vision**

Michael Albert

149

planning, a system in which worker and consumer councils propose their work activities and consumer preferences in light of accurate knowledge of local and global implications and true valuations of the full social benefits and costs their choices will impose and garner.

The participatory planning system utilises a back and forth cooperative communication of mutually informed preferences via a variety of simple communicative and organising principles and vehicles including indicative prices, facilitation boards, and rounds of accommodation to new information—all permitting actors to express and to mediate and refine their desires in light of feedback about other's desires, and to arrive at compatible choices consistent with remuneration for effort and sacrifice, balanced job complexes, and participatory self-managing influence.

Is the above a full picture of an economic alternative to capitalism? Of course not—it is way too brief. But within the limits of available space, it is hopefully provocative and inspiring. Participatory economics includes:

- Self-managing workplace and consumer councils for equitable participation
- Diverse decision-making procedures seeking proportionate say for those affected by decisions
- Balanced job complexes creating just distribution of empowering and disempowering circumstances
- Remuneration for effort and sacrifice in accord with worthy moral and economic logic
- Participatory planning in tune with economics serving human wellbeing and development

Together these features constitute the core institutional scaffolding of participatory economics, an institutional alternative to capitalism and also to what has been called centrally planned or market socialism but which really should be called coordinatorism. Are there fuller formulations of this particular economic vision's morality and its logic? Most certainly there are. If interested, consult the parecon site at www.parecon.org. It includes articles, interviews, whole books and further references. But for now, in this space, we need to ask what implications would advocating participatory economics have for our current movement work?

Just before getting on to strategy, however, I should say that in my view economic vision and agenda is not enough. I am emphasising economics because it is my main area of investigation and because the assignment for this book was to address capitalism. But we also need political, cultural and gender-related vision and agenda. Our positive movements should not just be anti-capitalist and not even that plus pro participatory economics in its place. They should also be anti authoritarian, anti racist, and anti sexist, and they should be pro a new political, cultural, and kinship vision as well.

Pareconish strategy

When we struggle for change we are generally trying to win changes which improve people's lives in the present and auger still more improvements in the future, or we are trying to develop our means to do so by raising consciousness and building projects and movements.

If we do all this with the intent of attaining a new system, it is revolutionary. If we do it assuming that the systemic features around us are permanent, it is reformist.

So, opposing capitalism and advocating parecon, my first strategic implication is that we ought to be fighting for changes in the present or building means to win more changes in the future all in a manner that leads toward a whole new system rather than presuming replication of this one.

This means our choices of issues to fight around and even more our choices of how to discuss those issues and develop consciousness bearing on them and our means of galvanising our energies into lasting movement forms has to move toward where we want to wind up.

Fighting for better wages or distribution of income we should be developing awareness of and support for remuneration for effort and sacrifice. Fighting for better conditions and quality of life at work, we should be developing awareness of and support for balanced job complexes. Fighting for a say over outcomes in workplaces or the national budget, we should be developing awareness of and support for participatory planning. As venues of struggle we ought to be building workers' and consumers' councils, when able. The choice of demands but also methods and content of our acts should all be influenced by our goals.

There is also an overarching issue. Seeking classlessness we must not have a movement that perpetuates class division and that empowers what I call a coordinator class while disempowering the working class. This advisory, taken seriously, would over time impact virtually the entire array of choices that face activists.

For example, our own organisations should be as classless as we can now make them, our decision making should be as self-managing as we can now make it—and likewise our divisions of labour should be as classless as we can now make them, which is to say they should incorporate balanced job complexes and self-management. In other words, if we seek parecon, we should not build alternative institutions and movements that replicate capitalist divisions of labour and modes of decision making—just as if we are against racism or sexism we should not build movements that perpetuate these ills via their cultures, roles, etc. Instead, regarding the class issue we should seek to progressively incorporate pareconish structures and norms such as self-management, councils, participation, equitable remuneration, and balanced job complexes, and regarding race and gender we should progressively work toward anti-racist and anti-sexist structures and norms. We can't do it all overnight, nor should we be apocalyptic about it, but if we sincerely seek a better world, anything less than this direction of innovation is not only hypocritical, it is suicidal due to disempowering and even alienating constituencies who must define and win that world. In other words, an additional major strategic insight of a participatory economic viewpoint is that we need to incorporate classless values and structures in our demands, our process, or projects, and our movements.

We ought to fight for changes in the present in a manner that leads toward a whole new system

Michael Albert

153

But, beyond that, how come past anti-capitalist struggles that sought socialism, and that won, have instead universally mired down with authoritarian dictatorships, homogenised cultures, patriarchal kin systems, and alienated, polluted and class-divided economies?

The answer is because in their concepts and strategies, despite the wishes of most of their grassroots adherents, that's what those prior movements aimed for. Anti-capitalist revolutions have not failed to produce self-managing societies due to inexorable laws of social organisation or of human inadequacy. The problem was instead within them. The movements succeeded in their goals, but succeeding meant instituting what their commitments implied: one party political rule, coordinator-ruled economies, and also homogenised cultures and still patriarchal kinship relations. It was not fate or nature or physics or even the aspirations of the great mass of their members that prevented these past efforts from being fully liberating. It was their strategies which were aimed at and successfully attained outcomes contrary to what most of the participants hoped for. Thus another major strategic insight of having participatory economic goals is that we need to say goodbye to Leninist strategic blindness to or support for coordinator domination and statist authoritarianism, and to organise for short- and long-term aims using organisational forms and methodologies that really do accord with our highest aspirations.

For example, imagine diverse movements each of which offer direction for their focused area—gender, race, economy, ecology, war and peace, etc—but which take their lead from other movements regarding focuses beyond what they directly prioritise. Call this entire conglomeration a movement of movements where the total project is the total sum of all the parts rather than a least common denominator coalition of them.

Imagine also an electoral component that is beholden to the grassroots activists and democratically organised and empowered. And imagine parallel and entwined efforts to create grassroots councils in workplaces and neighbourhoods, in turn seen as the infrastructure of a new type economy to come.

Imagine too demands for diverse immediate improvements all sought not as ends in themselves but as steps toward a new society. Each new demand for better pay and income distribution, for a shorter work week, for affirmative action, for better voting rules, for more power at work, for changes in military budgeting and foreign policies, for participatory budgeting, for replacing the IMF, World Bank and World Trade Organisation, for establishing a world parliament, and many more gains, is sought in ways that leave movements larger, more committed, more intent on continued struggle, and structurally better able to empower workers, women, minorities and all subordinate citizens, rather than in ways that quickly suffer roll-back or become dominated by elites.

We need to move from exclusively indicating what is wrong with society to advocating what we desire

Michael Albert

155

And imagine as well a sustained, reasoned and patient commitment to incorporate in our work the features we seek for a new society such as balanced job complexes, self-management, feminism, multiculturalism, political participation, etc, both so that we learn more about these aims, and also to demonstrate their worth in order to meet needs, inspire desire and provide hope.

What impedes doing all of this is not the power of the state or the ubiquity of manipulative mass media. These are huge factors, of course. But they are a given. That's the world we operate in. The key variable over which we have influence is ourselves. We need to move from exclusively indicating what is wrong with society to largely advocating what we desire for society. And we need to stop incorporating contemporary societal assumptions that we hate in our projects, and to instead start implementing those we favour.

Viewed with one disposition, history has so far been a horrible accumulation of oppression and suffering. Viewed with another disposition, however, history has chronicled humans discovering their own finer potentials and together mounting heroic offensives to attain them—against monarchy, feudalism, slavery, Jim Crow racism, apartheid, sexual subjugation, second class citizenship, sexism, heterosexism, dictatorship, one-party rule, capitalism and coordinatorism (calling itself socialism)—and seeking, in their place, equity, justice and freedom. The gains humans have made have been steady and plentiful. Now a major leap is possible. Consistent with past efforts, we can now attain fully liberatory goals, including, I think, participatory economics and also alternative structures for polity, culture and kinship. We have only to make the effort.

To order more copies of this book **contact**

Bookmarks Publications Ltd
1 Bloomsbury Street
London WC1B 3QE
020 7637 1848
www.bookmarks.uk.com
publications@bookmarks.uk.com

Also available:

Anti-capitalism
A Guide to the Movement

Anti-imperialism
A Guide for the Movement